HUDSON TAYLOR'S
SPIRITUAL SECRET

HUDSON TAYLOR'S SPIRITUAL SECRET

By

DR. AND MRS. HOWARD TAYLOR

Authors of *Hudson Taylor,* in two vols.:

The Growth of a Soul

The Growth of a Work of God

MOODY PRESS
CHICAGO

ISBN 0-8024-0029-9

33 34 35 36 37 Printing/LC/Year 87 86 85 84 83 82

Printed in the United States of America

To our father's dear and honored friend
DR. HENRY W. FROST
for forty-two years Director in North America
of the China Inland Mission:
with the love of two generations

FOREWORD

THIS RECORD has been prepared especially for readers unfamiliar with the details of Mr. Hudson Taylor's life. Those who have read the larger biography by the present writers, or Mr. Marshall Broomhall's more recent presentation, will find little that is new in these pages. But there are many, in the western world especially, who have hardly heard of Hudson Taylor, who have little time for reading and might turn away from a book in two volumes, yet who need and long for just the inward joy and power that Hudson Taylor found.

The desire of the writers is to make available to busy people the experiences of their beloved father—thankful for the blessing brought to their own lives by what he was, and what he found in God, no less than by his fruitful labours.

HOWARD AND GERALDINE TAYLOR

Philadelphia,
May 21, 1932

Men are God's method. The church is looking for better methods; God is looking for better men. . . . What the church needs today is not more machinery or better, not new organizations or more and novel methods, but men whom the Holy Ghost can use—men of prayer, men mighty in prayer. The Holy Ghost does not come on machinery, but on men. He does not anoint plans, but men—men of prayer. . . .

The training of the Twelve was the great, difficult and enduring work of Christ. . . . It is not great talents or great learning or great preachers that God needs, but men great in holiness, great in faith, great in love, great in fidelity, great for God—men always preaching by holy sermons in the pulpit, by holy lives out of it. These can mold a generation for God.

E. M. Bounds

The founder of the China Inland Mission was a physician, J. Hudson Taylor, a man full of the Holy Ghost and of faith, of entire surrender to God and His call, of great self-denial, heartfelt compassion, rare power in prayer, marvelous organizing faculty, energetic initiative, indefatigable perseverance, and of astonishing influence with men, and withal of childlike humility.

PROFESSOR WARNECK

Surely never was man better fitted for his work than he for the difficult undertaking of founding and conducting a great interdenominational and international mission in million-peopled China. The China Inland Mission was conceived in his soul, and every stage of its advance sprang from his personal exertions. In the quiet of his heart, in deep unutterable communings with God, the Mission had its origin, and it remains his memorial.

H. GRATTAN GUINNESS, D.D.

CONTENTS

1

AN OPEN SECRET

Bear not a single care thyself,
One is too much for thee;
The work is Mine, and Mine alone;
Thy work—to rest in Me.

—SELECTED

HUDSON TAYLOR was no recluse. He was a man of affairs, the father of a family, and one who bore large responsibilities. Intensely practical, he lived a life of constant change among all sorts and conditions of men. He was no giant in strength, no Atlas to bear the world upon his shoulders. Small in stature and far from strong, he had always to face physical limitations. Next to godly parentage, the chief advantage of his early years was that he had to support himself from the time he was about sixteen. He became a hard worker and an efficient medical man; he was able to care for a baby, cook a dinner, keep accounts, and comfort the sick and sorrowing, no less than to originate great enterprises and afford spiritual leadership to thoughtful men and women the wide world over.

Above all, he put to the test the promises of God, and proved it possible to live a consistent spiritual life on the highest plane. He overcame difficulties such as few men have ever had to encounter, and left a work which long after his death is still growing in extent and usefulness. Inland China opened to the Gospel largely as an outcome of this life, tens of thousands of souls won to Christ in previously unreached provinces, twelve hundred missionaries depending upon God for the supply of all their needs without promise of salary, a mission which has never made an appeal for financial help, yet has never been in debt, that never asks man or woman to join its ranks, yet has sent to China recently two hundred new workers given in answer to prayer — such is the challenge that calls us to emulate Hudson Taylor's faith and devotion.

What was the secret, we may well ask, of such a life? Hudson Taylor had many secrets, for he was always going on with God, yet they were but one — the simple, profound secret of drawing for every need, temporal or spiritual, upon "the fathomless wealth of Christ." To find out how he did this, and to make our own his simple, practical attitude toward spiritual things, would solve our problems and ease our burdens, so that we too might become all that God would make us. We want, we need, we may have Hudson Taylor's secret and his success, for we have Hudson Taylor's Bible and his God.

Remember them that have the rule over you . . .
and considering the issue of their life,
imitate their faith.
Jesus Christ is the same
yesterday and to-day, yea and forever.

2

SOUL-GROWTH IN EARLY YEARS

Turn your eyes upon Jesus,
   Look full in His wonderful face;
And the things of earth will grow strangely dim
   In the light of His glory and grace.

—H. LEMMEL

THE BEGINNING of it all was a quiet hour among his father's books, when young Hudson Taylor sought something to interest him. His mother was away from home and the boy was missing her. The house seemed empty, so he took the story he found to a favorite corner in the old warehouse, thinking he would read it as long as it did not get prosy.

Many miles away, the mother was specially burdened that Saturday afternoon about her only son. Leaving her friends she went alone to plead with God for his salvation. Hour after hour passed while that mother was still upon her knees, until her heart was flooded with a joyful assurance that her prayers were heard and answered.

The boy was reading, meanwhile, the booklet he

16

had picked up, and as the story merged into something more serious he was arrested by the words: "The finished work of Christ." Who can explain the mystery of the Holy Spirit's working? Truth long familiar, though neglected, came back to mind and heart.

"Why does the writer use those words?" he questioned. "Why does he not say, 'the atoning or propitiatory work of Christ'?"

Immediately, *It is finished* shone out as in letters of light. Finished? What was finished?

"A full and perfect atonement for sin," his heart replied. "The debt was paid by the great Substitute. 'Christ died for our sins,' and 'not for ours only, but also for the sins of the whole world.'"

Then came the thought with startling clearness, "If the whole work is finished, the whole debt paid, what is there left for me to do?"

The one, the only answer took possession of his soul: "There was nothing in the world for me to do save to fall upon my knees and accepting this Saviour and His salvation to praise Him for evermore."

Old doubts and fears were gone. The reality of the wonderful experience we call conversion filled him with peace and joy. New life came with that simple acceptance of the Lord Jesus Christ, for to "as many as received him, to them gave he power to become the sons of God." And great was the change that new life brought.

Longing to share his new-found joy with his

mother, he was the first to welcome her on her return.

"I know, my boy, I know," she said with her arms about him. "I have been rejoicing for a fortnight in the glad news you have to tell."

Another surprise awaited him not long after, when, picking up a notebook he thought was his own, he found an entry in his sister's writing to the effect that she would give herself daily to prayer until God should answer in the conversion of her only brother. The young girl had recorded this decision just a month previously.

> Brought up in such a circle [Hudson Taylor wrote] and saved under such circumstances, it was perhaps natural that from the very commencement of my Christian life I was led to feel that the promises of the Bible are very real, and that prayer is in sober fact transacting business with God, whether on one's own behalf or on behalf of those for whom one seeks His blessing.

The brother and sister were now one in a new way, and young though they were, for he was only seventeen, they began to do all they could to win others to Christ. This was the secret of the rapid growth which followed in spiritual things. They entered from the very first into the Lord's own yearning of heart over the lost and perishing. Not "social service," but living for others with a supreme concern for their soul's salvation was the line on which they were led out. And this not with any sense of superiority, but simply from a deep, personal love to the Lord Jesus Christ.

It was that love that as the days went on made it such a keen distress to fail in the old ways and lose the joy of His conscious presence. For there were ups and down as with most young Christians, and neglect of prayer and of feeding on God's Word always brings coldness of heart. But the outstanding thing about Hudson Taylor's early experience was that he could not be satisfied with anything less than the best, God's best—the real and constant enjoyment of His presence. To go without this was to live without sunlight, to work without power. That he knew the joy of the Lord in those early days is evident from recollections such as the following. A leisure afternoon had brought opportunity for prayer, and moved by deep longings he sought his room to be alone with God.

Well do I remember how in the gladness of my heart I poured out my soul before God. Again and again confessing my grateful love to Him who had done everything for me, who had saved me when I had given up all hope and even desire for salvation, I besought Him to give me some work to do for Him as an outlet for love and gratitude. . . .

Well do I remember as I put myself, my life, my friends, my all upon the altar, the deep solemnity that came over my soul with the assurance that my offering was accepted. The presence of God became unutterably real and blessed, and I remember . . . stretching myself on the ground and lying there before Him with unspeakable awe and unspeakable joy. For what service I was accepted I knew not, but a deep consciousness that I was not my own took possession of me which has never since been effaced.

If we think that boys or girls in their teens are too young for such soul-experiences, we are indeed mistaken. At no time in life is there greater capacity for devotion, if the heart's deepest springs are open to the love of Christ.

3

FIRST STEPS OF FAITH

And evermore beside him on his way
The unseen Christ shall move;
That he may lean upon His arm and say,
"Dost Thou, dear Lord, approve?"
—H. W. LONGFELLOW

IT WAS NO PERFECT BEING to whom this sense of call had come. A normal boy living a busy life, whether as clerk in a bank or assistant in his father's store, he had many temptations, and when a lively cousin came to be his roommate it was not easy to keep first things first and make time for prayer. Yet without this there cannot but be failure and unrest. The soul that is starved cannot rejoice in the Lord, and Hudson Taylor had to learn that there is no substitute for real spiritual blessing.

"I saw Him and I sought Him, I had Him and I wanted Him," wrote one who had gone far in the knowledge of God; and the Barnsley lad, though only at the beginning, had the same blessed hunger and thirst which the Lord loves to fill. "My soul

21

thirsteth for thee," was the longing of David. "My soul shall be satisfied," yet in the very same breath, "my soul followeth hard after thee."

It was in one such experience of defeat, longing and deeper blessing that the touch of God came to Hudson Taylor in a new way. In a moment and without a spoken word, he understood.

He had come to an end of himself, to a place where God only could deliver, where he *must* have His succor, His saving strength. If God would but work on his behalf, would break the power of sin, giving him inward victory in Christ, he would renounce all earthly prospects, he would go anywhere, do anything, suffer whatever His cause might demand and be wholly at His disposal. This was the cry of his heart, if God would but sanctify him and keep him from falling.

> Never shall I forget [he wrote long after] the feeling that came over me then. Words could not describe it. I felt I was in the presence of God, entering into a covenant with the Almighty. I felt as though I wished to withdraw my promise but could not. Something seemed to say, "Your prayer is answered; your conditions are accepted." And from that time the conviction has never left me that I was called to China.

China, that great country familiar to him from childhood through his father's prayers; China, to which he had been dedicated even before birth; China, whose need and darkness had often called him from afar—was that indeed God's purpose for his life? Distinctly, as if a voice had spoken, the word came in the silence, "Then go for Me to China."

From that moment life was unified in one great purpose and prayer. For Hudson Taylor was "not disobedient to the heavenly vision," and to him obedience to the will of God was a very practical matter. At once he began to prepare, as well as he could, for a life that would call for physical endurance. He took more exercise in the open air, exchanged his feather bed for a hard mattress and was watchful not to be self-indulgent at table. Instead of going to church twice on Sunday, he gave up the evening to visiting in the poorest parts of the town, distributing tracts and holding cottage meetings. In crowded lodging-house kitchens he became a welcome figure, and even on the race course his bright face and kindly words opened the way for many a straight message. All this led to more Bible study and prayer, for he soon found that there is One and One alone who can make us "fishers of men."

The study of Chinese, also, was entered upon with ardor. A grammar of that formidable language would have cost more than twenty dollars and a dictionary at least seventy-five. He could afford neither. But with a copy of the Gospel of Luke in Chinese, by patiently comparing brief verses with their equivalent in English, he found out the meaning of more than six hundred characters. These he learned and made into a dictionary of his own, carrying on at the same time other lines of study.

> I have begun to get up at five in the morning [he wrote to his sister at school] and find it necessary to go to bed early. I must study if I mean to go to China. I am fully decided to go, and am making every preparation I can. I intend to rub up my Latin, to learn Greek and the rudiments of Hebrew, and get as much general information as possible. I need your prayers.

Several years with his father as a dispensing chemist had increased his desire to study medicine, and when an opportunity occurred of becoming assistant to a leading physician in Hull he was not slow to avail himself of it. This meant leaving the home circle, but first in the doctor's residence and later in the home of an aunt, his mother's sister, the young assistant was still surrounded with refinement and comfort.

This proved, indeed, one of the elements in the new life which led him to serious thinking. Dr. Hardey paid a salary sufficient to cover personal expenses, but Hudson Taylor was giving, as a matter of duty and privilege, a tenth of all that came to him to the work of God. He was devoting time on Sunday to evangelism in a part of the town where there was urgent need for temporal as well as spiritual help. And this raised the question, why should he not spend less for himself and have the joy of giving more to others?

On the outskirts of the town, beyond some vacant

lots, a double row of cottages bordered a narrow
canal which gave the name of "Drainside" to the
none-too-attractive neighborhood. The canal was
just a deep ditch into which Drainside people were
in the habit of throwing rubbish to be carried away,
in part, whenever the tide rose high enough—for
Hull is a seaport town. The cottages, like peas in
a pod, followed the windings of the Drain for half
a mile or so, each having one door and two windows. It was for a rented room in one of these little places that Hudson Taylor left his aunt's pleasant home on Charlotte Street. Mrs. Finch, his landlady, was a true Christian and delighted to have
"the young doctor" under her roof. She did her
best, no doubt, to make the chamber clean and comfortable, polishing the fireplace opposite the window and making up the bed in the corner farthest
from the door. A plain deal table and a chair or
two completed the appointments. The room was
only twelve feet square and did not need much
furniture. It was on a level with the ground and
opened familiarly out of the kitchen. From the
window one looked across to "The Founder's Arms,"
a countrified public house whose lights were useful
on dark nights shining across the mud and water
of the Drain.

Whatever it may have been in summer, toward
the close of November when Hudson Taylor made
it his home Drainside must have seemed dreary
enough. To add to the changed conditions he was
boarding himself, which meant that he bought his

meager supplies as he returned from the surgery and rarely sat down to a proper meal. His walks were solitary, his evenings spent alone, and Sundays brought long hours of work in his district or among the crowds who frequented the Humber Dock.

Having now the twofold object in view [he recalled] of accustoming myself to endure hardness, and of economizing in order to help those among whom I was laboring in the Gospel, I soon found that I could live upon very much less than I had previously thought possible. Butter, milk and other luxuries I ceased to use, and found that by living mainly on oatmeal and rice, with occasional variations, a very small sum was sufficient for my needs. In this way I had more than two-thirds of my income available for other purposes, and my experience was that the less I spent on myself and the more I gave to others, the fuller of happiness and blessing did my soul become.

For God is no man's debtor, and here in his solitude Hudson Taylor was learning something of what He can be to the one who follows hard after Him. In these days of easy-going Christianity, is it not well to remind ourselves that it really does *cost* to be a man or woman whom God can use? One cannot obtain a Christlike character for nothing; one cannot do a Christlike work save at great price. "Can ye drink of the cup that I drink of, and be baptized with the baptism wherewith I am baptized?"

China was occupying no little public attention at

this time, because of the remarkable developments of the Taiping Rebellion. Many were praying, and countless hearts were more or less stirred about its evangelization. But when disappointment came, and the failure of enterprises that promised well, the majority ceased to help or care. Prayer meetings dwindled to nothing, would-be missionaries turned to other callings, and contributions dropped off to such an extent that more than one society actually ceased to exist. But here and there were those upon whom the Lord could count—poor and weak perhaps, unknown and unimportant, but ready, by grace, to go all lengths in carrying out His purposes.

Here in his quiet lodging at Drainside was such a man. With all his limitations, Hudson Taylor desired supremely a Christlike character and life. As test came after test that might have been avoided, he chose the pathway of self-emptying and the cross, not from any idea of merit in so doing, but simply because led by the Spirit of God. Thus he was in an attitude that did not hinder blessing.

"Behold I have set before thee an open door, and no man can shut it; for thou hast a little strength, and hast kept my word, and has not denied my name."

"A great door and effectual . . . and there are many adversaries."

Adversaries there certainly were to oppose Hudson Taylor's progress at this time. He was entering upon one of the most fruitful periods of his life, rich in blessing for himself and others. Is it any wonder that the tempter was at hand? He was alone, hungry for love and sympathy, living a life of self-denial not easy for a lad to bear. It was just the opportunity for the Devil, and he was permitted for a while to do his worst, that even that might be overruled for good.

For it was just at this juncture, when he had been at Drainside only a few weeks, that the dreaded blow fell, and the one he loved with a great love seemed lost to him forever. For two long years he had hoped and waited. The very uncertainty of the future made him long the more for her presence, her companionship through all changes. But now the dream was over. Seeing that nothing could dissuade her friend from his missionary purpose, the young music teacher—with her sweet face and lovely voice—made it plain at last that she was not prepared to go to China. Her father would not hear of it, nor did she feel fitted for such a life. This could mean but one thing, though the heart that loved her best was well-nigh broken.

"Is it all worth while?" urged the tempter. "Why should you go to China, after all? Why toil and suffer all your life for an ideal of duty? Give it up now, while you can yet win her. Earn a proper living like everybody else, and serve the Lord at home. For you *can* win her yet."

Love pleaded hard. It was a moment of wavering. The enemy came in like a flood, for the lad was benumbed with sorrow, and instead of turning to the Lord for comfort he kept it to himself and nursed his grief. But he was not forsaken.

Alone in the surgery [he wrote the following day] I had a melting season. I was thoroughly softened and humble, and had a wonderful manifestation of the love of God. "A broken and a contrite heart" He did not despise, but answered my cry for blessing in very deed and truth.

Yes, He has humbled me and shown me what I am, revealing Himself as a present, a very present help in time of trouble. And though He does not deprive me of feeling in my trial, He enables me to sing, "Yet will I rejoice in the Lord, I will joy in the God of my salvation." . . .

Now I am happy in my Saviour's love. I can thank Him for *all*, even the most painful experiences of the past, and trust Him without fear for all that is to come.

4

FURTHER STEPS OF FAITH

Who trust in God's unchanging love
Build on the rock that nought can move.
—NEUMARK

I NEVER MADE a sacrifice," said Hudson Taylor in later years, looking back over a life in which that element was certainly not lacking. But what he said was true, for the compensations were so real and lasting that he came to see that giving up is inevitably receiving, when one is dealing heart to heart with God. It was so, very manifestly, this winter at Drainside. Not outwardly only but inwardly also he had accepted the will of God, giving up what seemed his best and highest, the love that had become part of his very life, that he might be unhindered in following Christ. The sacrifice was great, but the reward far greater.

Unspeakable joy [he tells us] all day long and every day, was my happy experience. God, even my God, was a living bright reality, and all I had to do was joyful service.

A new tone was perceptible about his letters

which were less introspective from this time onward and more full of missionary purpose. China came to the front again in all his thinking, and there was deeper soul-exercise over the spiritual condition of those out of Christ.

Do not let anything unsettle you, dear Mother [he wrote about this time]. Missionary work is indeed the noblest any mortal can engage in. We certainly cannot be insensible to the ties of nature, but should we not rejoice when we have anything we can give up for the Saviour? . . .

Continue to pray for me. Though comfortable as regards temporal matters, and happy and thankful, I feel I need your prayers. . . . Oh, Mother, I cannot tell you, I cannot describe how I long to be a missionary; to carry the Glad Tidings to poor, perishing sinners; to spend and be spent for Him who died for me! . . . Think, Mother, of twelve millions—a number so great that it is impossible to realize it—yes, twelve million souls in China, every year, passing without God and without hope into eternity. . . . Oh, let us look with compassion on this multitude! God has been merciful to us; let us be like Him. . . .

I must conclude. Would you not give up *all* for Jesus who died for you? Yes, Mother, I know you would. God be with you and comfort you. Must I leave as soon as I can save money enough to go? I feel as if I could not live if something is not done for China.

Yet much as he longed to go and go at once, there were considerations that held him back. The little room at Drainside witnessed many a conflict and victory known to God alone.

To me it was a very grave matter [he wrote of that winter] to contemplate going out to China, far from all human aid, there to depend upon the living God alone for protection, supplies and help of every kind. I felt that one's spiritual muscles required strengthening for such an undertaking. There was no doubt that if faith did not fail, God would not fail. But what if one's faith should prove insufficient? I had not at that time learned that even "if we believe not, yet he abideth faithful; he cannot deny himself." It was consequently a very serious matter to my mind, not whether He was faithful, but whether I had strong enough faith to warrant my embarking on the enterprise set before me.

"When I get out to China," I thought to myself, "I shall have no claim on anyone for anything. My only claim will be on God. How important to learn, before leaving England, to move man, through God, by prayer alone."

And for this he was willing to pay the price, whatever it might be. There may have been some lack of judgment, perhaps some going to extremes, but how wonderfully God understood and met him! "To move man, through God, by prayer alone"—it was a great ambition, gloriously realized that lonely winter at Drainside.

At Hull my kind employer [he continued] wished me to remind him whenever my salary became due. This I determined not to do directly, but to ask that God would bring the fact to his recollection, and thus encourage me by answering prayer.

At one time, as the day drew near for the payment of a quarter's salary, I was as usual much in prayer about it. The time arrived but Dr. Hardey made no allusion to the matter. I continued praying. Days passed on and he did not remember, until at length on settling up my weekly accounts one Saturday night, I found myself possessed of only one remaining coin—a half-crown piece.[1] Still, I had hitherto known no lack, and I continued praying.

That Sunday was a very happy one. As usual my heart was full and brimming over with blessing. After attending divine service in the morning, my afternoons and evenings were taken up with Gospel work in the various lodging-houses I was accustomed to visit in the lowest part of the town. At such times it almost seemed to me as if heaven were begun below, and that all that could be looked for was an enlargement of one's capacity for joy, not a truer filling than I possessed.

After concluding my last service about ten o'clock that night, a poor man asked me to go and pray with his wife, saying that she was dying. I readily agreed, and on the way asked him why he had not sent for the priest, as his accent told me he was an Irishman. He had done so, he said, but the priest refused to come without a payment of eighteen pence, which the man did not possess as the family was starving. Immediately it occurred to my mind that all the money I had in the world was the solitary half-crown, and that it was in one coin; moreover, that while the basin of water-gruel I usually took for supper was awaiting me, and there was sufficient in the house for breakfast in the

1About the value of a dollar, at that time.

morning, I certainly had nothing for dinner on the coming day.

Somehow or other there was at once a stoppage in the flow of joy in my heart. But instead of reproving myself I began to reprove the poor man, telling him that it was very wrong to have allowed matters to get into such a state as he described, and that he ought to have applied to the relieving officer. His answer was that he had done so, and was told to come at eleven o'clock the next morning, but that he feared his wife might not live through the night.

"Ah," thought I, "if only I had two shillings and a sixpence instead of this half-crown, how gladly would I give these poor people a shilling!" But to part with the half-crown was far from my thoughts. I little dreamed that the truth of the matter simply was that I could trust God plus *one-and-sixpence,* but was not prepared to trust Him only, without any money at all in my pocket.

My conductor led me into a court, down which I followed him with some degree of nervousness. I had found myself there before, and at my last visit had been roughly handled. . . . Up a miserable flight of stairs into a wretched room he led me, and oh, what a sight there presented itself! Four or five children stood about, their sunken cheeks and temples telling unmistakably the story of slow starvation, and lying on a wretched pallet was a poor, exhausted mother, with a tiny infant thirty-six hours old moaning rather than crying at her side.

"Ah!" thought I, "if I had two shillings and a sixpence, instead of half-a-crown, how gladly should they have one-and-sixpence of it." But still a wretched unbelief prevented me from obeying the impulse to relieve their distress at the cost of all I possessed.

It will scarcely seem strange that I was unable to say much to comfort these poor people. I needed comfort myself. I began to tell them, however, that they must not be cast down; that though their circumstances were very distressing there was a kind and loving Father in heaven. But something within me cried, "You hypocrite! telling these un-converted people about a kind and loving Father in heaven, and not prepared yourself to trust Him without half-a-crown."

I nearly choked. How gladly would I have com-promised with conscience, if I had had a florin and a sixpence! I would have given the florin thankfully and kept the rest. But I was not yet prepared to trust in God alone, without the six-pence.

To talk was impossible under these circum-stances, yet strange to say I thought I should have no difficulty in praying. Prayer was a delightful occupation in those days. Time thus spent never seemed wearisome and I knew no lack of words. I seemed to think that all I should have to do would be to kneel down and pray, and that relief would come to them and to myself together.

"You asked me to come and pray with your wife," I said to the man; "let us pray." And I knelt down.

But no sooner had I opened my lips with, "Our Father who art in heaven," than conscience said within, "Dare you mock God? Dare you kneel down and call Him 'Father' with that half-crown in your pocket?"

Such a time of conflict then came upon me as I had never experienced before. How I got through that form of prayer I know not, and whether the words uttered were connected or disconnected. But I arose from my knees in great distress of mind.

The poor father turned to me and said, "You see what a terrible state we are in, sir. If you can help us, for God's sake do!"

At that moment the word flashed into my mind, "Give to him that asketh of thee." And in the word of a King there is power.

I put my hand into my pocket and slowly drawing out the half-crown gave it to the man, telling him that it might seem a small matter for me to relieve them, seeing that I was comparatively well off, but that in parting with that coin I was giving him my all; but that what I had been trying to tell them was indeed true, God really was a Father and might be trusted. And how the joy came back in full flood tide to my heart! I could say anything and feel it then, and the hindrance to blessing was gone—gone, I trust, forever.

Not only was the poor woman's life saved, but my life as I fully realized had been saved too. It might have been a wreck—would have been, probably, as a Christian life—had not grace at that time conquered and the striving of God's Spirit been obeyed.

I well remember that night as I went home to my lodgings how my heart was as light as my pocket. The dark, deserted streets resounded with a hymn of praise that I could not restrain. When I took my basin of gruel before retiring, I would not have exchanged it for a prince's feast. Reminding the Lord as I knelt at my bedside of His own Word, "He that giveth to the poor lendeth to the Lord," I asked Him not to let my loan be a long one, or I should have no dinner the next day. And with peace within and peace without, I spent a happy, restful night.

Next morning my plate of porridge remained for breakfast, and before it was finished the postman's knock was heard at the door. I was not in the habit of receiving letters on Monday, as my parents and most of my friends refrained from posting on Saturday, so that I was somewhat surprised when the landlady came in holding a letter or packet in her wet hand covered by her apron. I looked at the letter, but could not make out the handwriting. It was either a strange hand or a feigned one, and the postmark was blurred. Where it came from I could not tell. On opening the envelope I found nothing written within, but inside a sheet of blank paper was folded a pair of kid gloves from which, as I opened them in astonishment, half-a-sovereign fell to the ground.

"Praise the Lord," I exclaimed, "four hundred

per cent for a twelve hours' investment! How glad
the merchants of Hull would be if they could lend
their money at such a rate of interest!" Then and
there I determined that a bank that could not
break should have my savings or earnings as the
case might be, a determination I have not yet
learned to regret.

I cannot tell you how often my mind has re-
curred to this incident, or all the help it has been
to me in circumstances of difficulty. If we are faithful to God in little things, we shall gain experience
and strength that will be helpful to us in the more
serious trials of life.

But this was not the end of the story, nor was it
the only answer to prayer that was to confirm Hudson Taylor's faith at this time.

This remarkable and gracious deliverance was a
great joy to me as well as a strong confirmation of
faith. But of course ten shillings, however eco-
nomically used, will not go very far, and it was
none the less necessary to continue in prayer, asking that the larger supply which was still due might
be remembered and paid. All my petitions, however, appeared to remain unanswered, and before
a fortnight elapsed I found myself pretty much in
the same position that I had occupied on the Sunday night already made so memorable. Meanwhile
I continued pleading with God, more and more
earnestly, that He would Himself remind Dr.
Hardey that my salary was due.

Of course it was not want of money that distressed me. That could have been had at any time
for the asking. The question uppermost in my

mind was, "Can I go to China, or will my want
of faith and power with God prove so serious an
obstacle as to preclude my entering upon this
much-prized service?"

As the week drew to a close I felt exceedingly
embarrassed. There was not only myself to consider. On Saturday night a payment would be
due to my Christian landlady, which I knew she
could not well dispense with. Ought I not, for
her sake, to speak about the matter of the salary?
Yet to do so would be, to myself at any rate, the
admission that I was not fitted to undertake a
missionary enterprise. I gave nearly the whole of
Thursday and Friday, all the time not occupied
in my necessary employment, to earnest wrestling
with God in prayer. But still on Saturday morning I was in the same position as before. And now
my earnest cry was for guidance as to whether I
should still continue to wait the Father's time. As
far as I could judge, I received the assurance that
to wait His time was best, and that God in some
way or other would interpose on my behalf. So I
waited, my heart being now at rest and the burden
gone.

About five o'clock that Saturday afternoon, when
Dr. Hardey had finished writing his prescriptions,
his last circuit for the day being done, he threw
himself back in his armchair as he was wont and
began to speak of the things of God. He was a
truly Christian man, and many seasons of happy
fellowship we had together. I was busily watching at the time a pan in which a decoction was
boiling that required a good deal of attention. It

was indeed fortunate for me that it was so, for without any obvious connection with what had been going on, all at once he said:

"By the by, Taylor, is not your salary due again?"

My emotion may be imagined. I had to swallow two or three times before I could answer. With my eye fixed on the pan and my back to the doctor, I told him as quietly as I could that it was over-due some little time. How thankful I felt at that moment! God surely had heard my prayer and caused him in this time of my great need to re-member the salary, without any word or suggestion from me.

"Oh, I am so sorry you did not remind me," he replied. "You know how busy I am. I wish I had thought of it a little sooner, for only this after-noon I sent all the money I had to the bank. Otherwise I would pay you at once."

It is impossible to describe the revulsion of feel-ing caused by this unexpected statement. I knew not what to do. Fortunately for me the pan boiled up and I had a good reason for rushing with it from the room. Glad indeed I was to keep out of sight until after Dr. Hardey had returned to his house, and most thankful that he had not per-ceived my emotion.

As soon as he was gone, I had to seek my little sanctum and pour out my heart before the Lord before calmness, and more than calmness, thank-fulness and joy were restored. I felt that God had His own way and was not going to fail me. I had sought to know His will early in the day, and as far as I could judge had received guidance to wait patiently. And now God was going to work for me in some other way.

That evening was spent, as my Saturday evenings usually were, in reading the Word and preparing the subject on which I expected to speak in the various lodging-houses on the morrow. I waited perhaps a little longer than usual. At last about ten o'clock, there being no interruption of any kind, I put on my overcoat and was preparing to leave for home, rather thankful to know that by that time I should have to let myself in with the latchkey, as my landlady retired early. There was certainly no help for that night. But perhaps God would interpose for me by Monday, and I might be able to pay my landlady early in the week the money I would have given her before, had it been possible.

Just as I was about to turn down the gas, I heard the doctor's step in the garden that lay between the dwelling-house and surgery. He was laughing to himself heartily, as though greatly amused. Entering the surgery he asked for the ledger, and told me that, strange to say, one of his richest patients had just come to pay his doctor's bill. Was it not an odd thing to do! It never struck me that it might have any bearing on my own case, or I might have felt embarrassed. Looking at it simply from the position of an uninterested spectator, I also was highly amused that a man rolling in wealth should come after ten o'clock at night to pay a bill which he could any day have met by a check with the greatest ease. It appeared that, somehow or other, he could not rest with this on his mind,

and had been constrained to come at that unusual hour to discharge his liability.

The account was duly receipted in the ledger
and Dr. Hardey was about to leave, when suddenly
he turned and handing me some of the banknotes
just received, said to my surprise and thankfulness:

"By the by, Taylor, you might as well take these
notes. I have no change, but can give you the
balance next week."

Again I was left, my feelings undiscovered, to go
back to my little closet and praise the Lord with a
joyful heart that after all I might go to China.

5

FAITH TRIED AND STRENGTHENED

Enough that God my Father knows:—
Nothing this faith can dim.
He gives the very best to those
Who leave the choice with Him.

—Selected

"AFTER ALL, I might go to China!" But how many testings still lay ahead. The life that was to be exceptionally fruitful had to be rooted and grounded in God in no ordinary way.

London followed Hull, and there Hudson Taylor entered as a medical student at one of the great hospitals. He was still depending on the Lord alone for supplies, for though his father and the Society which ultimately sent him to China both offered to help with his expenses, he felt he must not lose the opportunity of further testing the promises of God. When he declined his father's generous offer, the home circle concluded that the Society was meeting his needs. It did undertake his fees at the London Hospital, and an uncle in Soho gave him a home for a few weeks, but beyond this there was nothing between him and want in the great city, save the faithfulness of God. Before leaving Hull he had written to his mother:

> I am indeed proving the truth of that word, "Thou wilt keep him in perfect peace whose mind is stayed on thee, because he trusteth in thee." My mind is quite as much at rest as, nay more than, it would be if I had a hundred pounds in my pocket. May He keep me ever thus, simply depending on Him for every blessing, temporal as well as spiritual.

And to his sister Amelia:

> No situation has turned up in London that will suit me, but I am not concerned about it, as HE is "the same yesterday, and today, and for ever." His love is unfailing, His Word unchangeable, His power ever the same; therefore the heart that trusts Him is kept in "perfect peace." . . . I know He tries me only to increase my faith, and that it is all in love. Well, if He is glorified, I am content.

For the future, near as well as distant, Hudson Taylor had one all-sufficient confidence. If that could fail, it were better to make the discovery in London than far away in China. Deliberately and of his own free will, he cut himself off from possible sources of supply. It was God, the living God he needed—a stronger faith to grasp His faithfulness, and more experience of the practicability of dealing with Him about every situation. Comfort or discomfort in London, means or the lack of means, seemed a small matter compared with deeper knowledge of the One on whom everything depends. Now that a further opportunity had come for putting that knowledge to the test, he did not hesitate, though he knew that no little trial might be involved.

The outcome proved that in this decision the young medical student was indeed led of God. Many and unmistakable were the answers to prayer in London which strengthened his faith, affording just the preparation needed for unforeseen developments which hastened his departure for China within the next twelve months. In his own brief *Retrospect* Mr. Taylor tells the story of these experiences.[1] Suffice it to say here, that the loneliness and privations that were permitted, the test of endurance—when for months together he lived on nothing but brown bread and apples, walking more than eight miles a day to and from the hospital—and all the uncertainty as to his connection with the one and only society prepared to send him to China without university training, went far to make him the man of faith he was even at this early age.

For Hudson Taylor was only twenty-one when the way opened unexpectedly, and he was requested by the Chinese Evangelization Society to sail for Shanghai as soon as a vessel could be found. The Taiping Rebellion had reached the zenith of its triumphant advance. With its capital firmly es-

---

[1] Write to: Overseas Missionary Fellowship, 404 South Church Street, Robesonia, Pennsylvania 19551.

tablished at Nanking, its nominally Christian forces
had swept over the central and northern provinces,
and Peking itself was almost within their grasp.
"Send me teachers, many teachers to help in making known the Truth," wrote their leader to an
American missionary whom he trusted.[2] "Here-
after, when my enterprise is successfully terminated,
I will disseminate the Doctrine throughout the
whole Empire, that all may return to the one Lord
and worship the true God only. This is what my
heart earnestly desires."

In a word, it seemed as though China would be
forthwith thrown open to messengers of the Gospel.
Christian hearts everywhere were deeply moved.
Something must be done and done at once to meet
so great a crisis, and for a time money poured into
the treasuries. Among other projects for advance,
the British and Foreign Bible Society undertook to
celebrate its Jubilee by printing a million copies of
the Chinese New Testament, and the society with
which Hudson Taylor was in correspondence de-

----

[2]This was Rev. F. J. Roberts of the American Baptist Missionary Union. Hung Siu-ts'uen, founder and leader of the
Taiping movement, first learned the Truth from a tract given
him during a literary examination in Canton by Liang A-fah,
one of Morrison's converts. Subsequently he returned to
Canton to hear more of the new Doctrine, and spent two or
three months in studying the Scriptures under the direction
of Mr. Roberts. Though he did not remain long enough to
be baptized and received into church fellowship, he had
learned enough of the spirit and teaching of Christianity to
make him a missionary to his own people on his return to
Kwangsi, the province in which his fervent propaganda began. It was not until bitter persecution from the Chinese
authorities had driven his followers to arms, that the movement took on a revolutionary character.

cided to send two men to Shanghai for work in the interior. One of these, a Scottish physician, could not leave immediately, but they counted upon the younger man to go at short notice, even though it meant sacrificing the degrees he was working for in medicine and surgery.

It was a serious step to take, and Hudson Taylor naturally turned to his parents for counsel and prayer. After an interview with one of the secretaries of the Chinese Evangelization Society he wrote to his mother:

> Mr. Bird has removed most of the difficulties I have been feeling, and I think it will be well to comply with his suggestion and at once propose myself to the Committee. I shall await your answer, and rely upon your prayers. If I should be accepted to go at once, would you advise me to come home before sailing? I long to be with you once more, and I know you would naturally wish to see me; but I almost think it would be easier for us not to meet, than having met to part again forever. No, not forever!
>
> "A little while: 'twill soon be past!
>   Why should we shun the promised cross?
> Oh, let us in His footsteps haste,
>   Counting for Him all else but loss:
> Then, how will recompense His smile
>   The sufferings of this little while!"
>
> I cannot write more, but hope to hear from you as soon as possible. Pray much for me. It is easy to talk of leaving all for Christ, but when it comes to the proof—it is only as we stand "complete in

Him" we can go through with it. God be with you
and bless you, my own dear Mother, and give you
so to realize the preciousness of Jesus that you may
wish for nothing but "to know him" . . . even in
"the fellowship of his sufferings."

And to his sister:

Pray for me, dear Amelia, that He who has
promised to meet all our need may be with me in
this painful though long-expected hour.

When we look at ourselves, at the littleness of
our love, the barrenness of our service and the
small progress we make toward perfection, how
soul-refreshing it is to turn away to Him; to plunge
afresh in "the fountain opened for sin and for un-
cleanness"; to remember that we are "accepted in
the beloved" . . . "who of God is made unto us
wisdom, and righteousness, and sanctification, and
redemption." Oh! the fulness of Christ, the fulness of Christ.

*   *   *   *   *

China in 1854, when after a perilous voyage of
five months Hudson Taylor first reached its shores,
was even more of a problem to the evangelist than
it is today. Shanghai and four other Treaty Ports
were the only places at which foreigners were allowed to reside, and there was not a single Protestant
missionary anywhere in the interior, i.e., away from
the coast. Civil war was raging, and the Taiping
propaganda had begun to lose its earlier character-
istics. Already it was degenerating into the corrupt
political movement which deluged the country with
blood and sufferings untold during the remaining

eleven years of its course. Instead of being able to reach Nanking and evangelize upcountry, Hudson Taylor had the greatest difficulty in gaining a foothold even in Shanghai, and only at the most serious risk could itinerations be undertaken.

Years afterwards, when responsible himself for the guidance of many missionaries, it was easy to see that the trials of those early days were all needed. He was pioneering a way in China, little as he or anyone else could imagine it, for hundreds who were to follow. Every burden must be his, every testing real as only experience can make it. As iron is tempered to steel, his heart must be stronger and more patient than others, through having loved and suffered more. He who was to encourage thousands in a life of childlike trust, must himself learn yet deeper lessons of a Father's loving care. So difficulties were permitted to gather about him, especially at first when impressions are deep and lasting, difficulties attended by many a deliverance which made them a lifelong blessing.

To begin with, Shanghai was in the grip of war. A band of rebels known as the "Red Turbans" was in possession of the native city, close to the Foreign Settlement, and forty to fifty thousand of the national forces were encamped round about. Fighting was almost continuous, and the foreign militia had frequently to be called out to protect the Settlement. Everything was at famine prices, and both the city and Settlement were so crowded that accommodation was scarcely to be obtained at any price. Had it not been that Dr. Lockhart of the London Mission was able to receive him for a time, the new arrival would have been hard put to it. Even so, sharp fighting was to be seen from his windows, and he was unable to walk in any direction without witnessing misery such as he had never dreamed of before.

It was also bitterly cold when Hudson Taylor first reached Shanghai, and as coal was selling at fifty dollars a ton it was not possible to do much to warm the houses. He was not accustomed to luxuries and was thankful for a shelter anywhere ashore but he suffered not a little from the penetrating chill and damp.

My position is a very difficult one [he wrote soon after his arrival]. Dr. Lockhart has taken me to reside with him for the present, as houses are not to be had for love or money. . . . No one can live in the city. . . . They are fighting now while I write, and the house shakes with the report of cannon.

It is so cold that I can hardly think or hold the pen. You will see from my letter to Mr. Pearse[3] how perplexed I am. It will be four months before I can hear in reply, and the very kindness of the missionaries who have received me with open arms makes me fear to be burdensome. Jesus will guide me aright. . . . I love the Chinese more than ever. Oh, to be useful among them!

Of his first Sunday in China he wrote:

---

[3] Secretary of the Chinese Evangelization Society, with Mr. Bird.

I attended two services at the London Mission and in the afternoon went into the city with Mr. Wylie. You have never seen a city in a state of siege. . . . God grant you never may! We walked some distance round the wall, and sad it was to see the wreck of rows upon rows of houses. Burnt down, blown down, battered to pieces—in all stages of ruin they were! And the misery of those who once occupied them and now, at this inclement season, are driven from home and shelter is terrible to think of. . . .

By the time we came to the North Gate they were fighting fiercely outside the city. One man was carried in dead, another shot through the chest, and a third whose arm I examined seemed in dreadful agony. A ball had gone clean through the arm breaking the bone in passing. . . . A little farther on we met some men bringing in a small cannon they had captured, and following them were others dragging along by their tails [queues] five wretched prisoners. The poor fellows cried to us piteously to save them as they were hurried by, but alas, we could do nothing! They would probably be at once decapitated. It makes one's blood run cold to think of such things.

The sufferings of those around him, and the fact that he could do little or nothing to help, would have been overwhelming, but for the strengthening of Him who suffers most.

What it means to be so far from home, at the seat of war [he added] and not able to understand or be understood by the people was fully realized.

Their utter wretchedness and misery and my in-
ability to help them or even point them to Jesus
powerfully affected me. Satan came in as a flood,
but there was One who lifted up a standard against
him. Jesus *is* here, and though unknown to the
majority and uncared-for by many who might know
Him, He is present and precious to His own.

Personal trials, too, were not lacking. For the
first time in his life, Hudson Taylor found himself
in a position in which he could hardly meet his
financial obligations. He had willingly lived on
next to nothing at home, to keep within his means,
but now he could not avoid expenses altogether beyond his income. Living with others who were receiving three or four times his salary, he was
obliged to board as they did, and saw his small
resources melt away with alarming rapidity. At
home he had been a collector for foreign missions,
and knew what it was to receive the hardly earned
contributions of the poor. Missionary money was
to him a sacred trust, and to have to use it so freely
caused him real distress. Then the letters he wrote
to the Society received but unsatisfactory replies.
After waiting months for instructions, he might hear
nothing at all in answer to his most urgent questions. The Committee in London was far away
and little able to understand his circumstances. They
were mostly busy men, absorbed in their own affairs, and with the best intentions and a real desire
to forward the work of God they were unable to
visualize a situation so different from anything they

had ever known. Hudson Taylor did his best to
make matters clear to them, but month after month
went by and he was left in uncertainty and financial
distress.

The Shanghai dollar, previously worth about fifty
cents gold, was up to twice that sum and continually rising higher, yet had no more purchasing value.
Obliged to exceed his salary for the necessaries of
life, he made use of a letter of credit provided against
emergencies but could not obtain any assurance that
his bills would be honored. It was a painful situation for one so conscientious in money matters, and
cost him many a wakeful night.

Then with the heat of summer came added per-
plexities. Not from his own Committee, but in a
roundabout way Hudson Taylor learned that the
Scotch physician who was to be his colleague had
already sailed from England with wife and children.
No instructions had reached him as to providing
accommodation for the family, and as the weeks
went by he realized that unless he took steps in the
matter they would be left without a roof over their
heads. Without authorization for such an expenditure, he had to find and rent rooms of some sort for
five people, and a difficult proposition it proved to
be. Not daring to afford a sedan chair—the proper
means of transport—he spent himself searching all
through city and Settlement, in the blinding heat
of August, for houses that were not to be had. His
Shanghai friends assured him that the only thing to
do was to buy land and build immediately. How

could he tell them the true situation or reveal his lack of funds? Criticism was already too current in the community as to the management of the society he represented; so he had to keep his troubles to himself, as far as possible, and seek to cast his burden upon the Lord.

> One who is really leaning on the Beloved [he wrote under these circumstances] finds it always possible to say, "I will fear no evil, for thou art with me." But I am so apt, like Peter, to take my eyes off the One to be trusted and look at the winds and waves. . . . Oh for more stability! The reading of the Word and meditation on the promises have been increasingly precious to me of late. At first I allowed my desire to acquire the language speedily to have undue prominence and a deadening effect on my soul. But now, in the grace that passes all understanding, the Lord has again caused His face to shine upon me.

And to his sister he added:

> I have been puzzling my brains again about a house, etc., but to no effect. So I have made it a matter of prayer, and have given it entirely into the Lord's hands, and now I feel quite at peace about it. He will provide and be my guide in this and every other perplexing step.

It must have seemed almost too good to be true when, only two days after the above was written, Hudson Taylor heard of premises that could be rented, and before the month was over found himself in possession of a house large enough to accommodate his expected colleagues. Five rooms upstairs and seven down seemed indeed a spacious residence. And though it was only a poor Chinese place, built of wood and very ramshackle, it was right among the people, near the North Gate of the city. Here then he established himself six months after his arrival in China, and though the situation was so dangerous that his teacher did not dare to go with him, he was able to engage a Shanghai Christian, an educated man, who could help him with the local dialect.

To be alone among the Chinese in a place of his own, and able, with the help of his new teacher, to carry on daily meetings and do a good deal of medical work, was joy indeed! But the location proved more perilous than he had anticipated. It was beyond the protection of the Settlement and within range of the Imperial artillery constantly covering the North Gate, so that it was not difficult to discover why the house had been left vacant. For almost three months the young missionary was able to hold on in the hope of some change for the better. But then the situation became desperate. His life had repeatedly been in danger, and he was obliged to witness day by day scenes of fiendish cruelty. At last the premises next door was set on fire with the intention of driving out the foreigner. No choice was left but to go back to the London Mission and there, just in time for the arrival of the Parkers, a refuge was found.

A little house on the London Missionary Society property, close to Dr. Lockhart's, had been the home

of Hudson Taylor's dearest friends in China. Often
had he shared their fireside, rejoicing in the happiness of the young English missionary and his wife.[4]
But with the coming of their first child the home
had been broken up and the father had taken his
motherless little one to the care of fellow-workers.
In his sorrow for his friend, Hudson Taylor had
not realized the bearing upon his own situation of
the empty house so rich in memories. But before
he had to leave his dangerous location near the
North Gate, the Burdon home was for rent. The
arrival of the Parkers was expected daily, and though
it left him with only three dollars in hand, Hudson
Taylor secured the house on his own responsibility,
just in time to receive his colleagues, including a
baby born at sea.

To help the situation he was glad to sublet half
the house to another missionary family in distress,
but that left only three rooms for the Parkers and
himself. Even so he was not able to furnish them
adequately, his few belongings making a poor show
when six people had to be provided for. But this
was only the beginning of troubles; for Dr. Parker,
too, had but a few dollars in hand, after the long
voyage by sailing ship, and was depending upon a
letter of credit from the Society, which by some mistake did not turn up. It was supposed to have been
sent off before the Parkers left England, but month
after month went by and there was no word of it

4Rev. J. S. Burdon of the Church Missionary Society, afterwards Bishop of Hongkong, for nearly fifty years a devoted and successful missionary in China.

or reference to its nonappearance. Not having been
led to expect severe winters, the family were in
sore need of warmer clothing and bedding. How
they lived at all through those trying months it is
hard to see, and the comments of the foreign community can easily be imagined.

Quietly Dr. and Mrs. Parker held on, not turned
aside from their missionary work by the tempting
possibilities open to a medical man in Shanghai.
He went out regularly with his young colleague
to evangelize in the city and surrounding villages,
and at home in their crowded quarters they devoted themselves assiduously to study. But all this
meant lessons burned into Hudson Taylor's heart
of how *not* to deal with those who, on the human
side, are dependent on one's care. The members of
the Committee in London were several of them
dear, personal friends of the missionaries. Fellowship with them in spiritual things, at Tottenham
and elsewhere, could never be forgotten, and even
when feeling their mistakes most keenly, Hudson
Taylor longed for their atmosphere of prayer and
love for the Word of God. But something somehow was wanting, and just what it was the young
missionary had to discover, that he might be practical as well as spiritual in his leadership in days to
come. So the iron, as with Joseph long ago, entered into his very soul; but from this endurance
was to spring heart's ease for many another.

You ask how I get over my troubles [he wrote
to his sister and intimate correspondent]. This is

the way. . . . I take them to the Lord. Since writing the above, I have been reading my evening portion—Psalms 72 to 74. Read them and see how applicable they are. I don't know how it is, but I can seldom read Scripture now without tears of joy and gratitude. . . .

I see that to be as I am and have been since my arrival has really been more conducive to improvement and progress than any other position would have been, though in many respects it has been painful and far from what I should myself have chosen. Oh, for more implicit reliance on the wisdom and love of God!

6

FRIENDSHIP AND SOMETHING MORE

Love that bent low beneath his brother's burden,
How shall he soar and find all sorrows flown!
Love that ne'er asked for answer or for guerdon,
How shall he meet eyes sweeter than his own!

—F. W. H. MEYERS

NOTHING IN THE RECORDS of his first two years in China is more surprising than the way in which Hudson Taylor devoted himself to pioneer evangelism. One might have thought that with the study of the language, amid war conditions and well-nigh overwhelmed as he was with other trials, he would scarcely have attempted frequent itinerations in what was then the interior. But to those years belong no fewer than ten evangelistic journeys all of which were more or less remarkable for their courage and endurance.

North, south, and west of Shanghai stretched a populous region made accessible by endless waterways. Junks were plentiful and afforded shelter of a sort at night, as well as transportation by day, so that travelers were not dependent on Chinese inns.

Simple cooking arrangements supplied food for the boatman's family and "guests," which might be supplemented by stores of one's own. The beds were just wooden boards and the tiny windows were often on a level with the floor, but one could lie down or sit on one's bedding when it was not possible to stand upright. Inconveniences were many, but people were made accessible in city after city, town after town, and villages never out of sight as one passed slowly along.

It was this that drew Hudson Taylor, as it had his Master long ago. The same "must" was in his heart: "I must work the works of him that sent me"; "I must preach the kingdom of God to other cities also"; "Other sheep I have, . . . them also I must bring." It was not enough to go to the highways and byways of Shanghai. Others were already doing that to some extent. His heart was burdened with a sense of responsibility for those *beyond*— those who never had heard the way of salvation, who never could hear unless the truth were brought to them by Christ-filled messengers. So nothing held him back, neither winter cold nor summer heat, nor even the peril of war conditions, which might endanger the lives of Europeans at any time or cut him off from return to Shanghai.

No sooner was one journey completed than he would start preparations for another. After a period devoted chiefly to study, he was familiar enough with the language to make himself understood in Mandarin as well as the local dialect, and the itinerations that followed were so intensive that these ten journeys were accomplished within fifteen months. Before Dr. Parker arrived, many excursions had been made to places within ten or fifteen miles of Shanghai, and during the first three months they were together, they distributed eighteen hundred New Testaments and Scripture portions and over two thousand explanatory books and tracts. These were given with the utmost care, only to those who could read, and as the majority were illiterate it meant covering a great deal of ground and explaining the message of the books to constantly changing crowds. Then, beginning in winter, four journeys were taken from January to March, in spite of zero weather, followed by others in April, May, June, August and September. Out among the crowds all day and in boats that had to be closed at night because of river thieves, there was little relief from the distressing heat. But nothing deterred the young evangelist.

The danger of these journeys was considerable, and when he was without companion the loneliness was keenly felt. Far from other foreigners, moving among not too friendly crowds, he quietly prosecuted his mission, finding his medical equipment of the greatest value in opening the way to people's hearts. His own heart, meanwhile, was entering more deeply into what it means to live and die "without Christ," and his outlook was enlarging. From temple-crowned hilltops and the height of ancient pagodas he would look down upon cities, towns and villages where the homes of millions of people were in sight—men, women and children who had never heard the one, the only Name "whereby we must be saved." Great thoughts, deep thoughts were moving in his heart, "thoughts lasting to the end."[1]

In the midst of it all, the civil war reached its desperate climax, and Shanghai fell before the Government forces. Hudson Taylor was traveling at the time with older missionaries toward the Soochow Lake. They had not been absent many days when they saw from the top of a hill the smoke of an immense conflagration. So great a fire in that direction could mean but one thing—Shanghai was in flames! And what of their families in the Settlement? Setting out at once to return, their fears were confirmed by fleeing rebels who sought protection. This of course the missionaries could not afford, and the men were caught and beheaded before their eyes. Hastening on with increasing ap-

---

[1] Long years after, on another journey, the last he ever took up the great Yangtze River, pacing the deck of the steamer in company with the writers he paused again and again, looking with misty eyes toward the hills on the southern shore. It was somewhere near Green Grass Island that he said at length:

"I wish I could tell you about it. It was over there, but I cannot remember just the spot."

Seeing him moved by some recollection we waited to hear more. But fifty years had passed since that day, the remembrance of which brought so deep a joy and awe. He could not put it into words. He tried but could not tell us what had been between his soul and God. But there, over there on those more distant heights it had come to him— some revelation of his future work, some call to utmost surrender for the life to which the Lord was leading—and its influence remained.

prehension, they came upon terrible evidences of the catastrophe that had taken place. But the Settlement was as they had left it. Satiated with slaughter, the Imperialists were too exultant over their conquest to pay much attention to foreigners.

Shanghai is now in peace [Hudson Taylor wrote], but it is like the peace of death. Two thousand people at the very least have perished, and the tortures some of the victims have undergone cannot have been exceeded by the worst barbarities of the Inquisition. The city is little more than a mass of ruins, and many of the wretched objects who survive are piteous to behold.

Still, the worst was over, and Hudson Taylor and his colleagues gave themselves to caring for the people, body and soul, while awaiting the reply of their Committee to suggestions for more settled work. Usefulness was what they longed for, and their plans had been well thought out and much prayed over. But the answer upon which their future seemed to depend was long in coming.

The heat of summer, meanwhile, was overpowering in their crowded quarters, and a brief visit to Ningpo opened a tempting prospect. For the missionaries in that city, feeling the need of a hospital to supplement their otherwise efficient organization, extended a cordial invitation to Dr. Parker to undertake this work, to which they pledged their united support. At this juncture, while still waiting the reply of their Committee, they received notice that the house they were sharing with another family would be needed shortly for members of the mission to which it belonged. Their fellow occupant was moving to premises of his own, but they had not been in a position to build, nor could they find rooms for rent anywhere in the Settlement or Chinese city. Only one course seemed open to Hudson Taylor, especially when the long-expected answer came and was unfavorable. The Committee was not prepared to spend money on building in the Ports. They wanted their workers to go to the interior, though where they were to live until that was feasible did not appear. Under these circumstances, Dr. and Mrs. Parker decided upon Ningpo, and their colleague was left in uncertainty. His friends gone, his home gone and no accommodation to be found even in the native city, how could he remain in Shanghai to carry on his work?

For a time he was much perplexed, but gradually out of these very difficulties emerged a new line of thought. He had been searching without success for any kind of place he could rent as a home base. The rapid influx of a new population made the housing problem in Shanghai more acute than ever. If he could not get a home on shore, why not take to boats as many Chinese do and live on the water? This would fit in well with the project he already had in mind of adopting Chinese dress, the better to prosecute his work. Yes, it all began to open up. He would take his few belongings to Ningpo, when he went to escort the Parkers, and would return to identify himself wholly with the people to whom his life was given.

But the step was not as simple as it seemed. Wearing Chinese dress in those days involved shaving the front part of the head and letting the hair grow long for the regulation queue. No missionary or other foreigner conformed to such a custom. For an occasional journey, a Chinese gown might be used over one's ordinary clothing, but to give up European dress and adopt the native costume altogether was quite another matter. Hudson Taylor had not been in China for a year and a half without realizing the social ostracism such action would involve. So for a time there was a struggle, though he was increasingly convinced of the wisdom of the step from a higher point of view.

It was access to the people he desired. A recent journey of twenty-five days alone, when he had penetrated two hundred miles up the Yangtze, had assured him that it was possible to do more than was generally supposed in itinerant evangelism. Of the fifty-eight towns and cities visited, fifty-one had never before been touched by messengers of the Gospel. But the weariness and strain of the journey had been largely due to the fact that he was wearing European clothing, the most outlandish costume to those who had never seen it before! Attention was continually distracted from his message by his appearance, which to his hearers was as undignified as it was comical. And after all, surely it mattered more to be suitably attired from the Chinese point

of view—when it was the Chinese he wanted to win—
rather than sacrifice their approval for that of the
small foreign community in the Ports. So the decision was come to at last, after much prayer and
searching the Word of God for guidance; and when
the Parkers were ready to leave for Ningpo, Hudson
Taylor's Chinese outfit was ready too, only waiting
the crucial moment when he would commit himself
to the barber's transforming hands.

It was an August evening when he went down to
the river to engage the junk that was to take the
Parkers on the first stage of their journey. On the
way a Chinese stranger accosted him, asking to his
surprise whether he was not seeking a house for
rent. Would a small one do, and in the Chinese
city? Because near the South Gate there was such
a house, only it was not quite finished building.
The owner had run short of money and did not
know how to complete the work. If the house suited,
no deposit would be asked, and it could probably
be had for an advance of six months' rent.

As if in a dream, Hudson Taylor followed his
guide to the southern part of the city, and there
found a small, compact house, perfectly new and
clean, with two rooms upstairs, two on the ground
floor, and a fifth across the courtyard for the servants,
just the thing he needed and in the locality he
would have chosen. What it meant to pay the
money over that night and secure the premises may
be better imagined than described. Then he had
not been mistaken after all! His work in Shanghai

was not finished. Prayer was being answered and the guidance given for which he had longed and waited.

That night he took the step which was to have so great an influence on the evangelization of inland China! When the barber had done his best, the young missionary darkened his remaining hair to match the long black braid which, at first, must do duty for his own. Then in the morning he put on as best he might the loose, unaccustomed garments, and appeared for the first time in the gown and satin shoes of the "Teacher," or man of the scholarly class.

Everything opened up after that in a new way. On the return journey to Shanghai he was not even recognized as a foreigner, until he began to preach or distribute books and see patients. Then women and children came around much more freely, and the crowds were less noisy and excited. While missing some of the prestige attaching to Europeans, he found it more than made up for by the freedom his changed appearance gave him in moving among the people. Their homes were open to him as never before, and it was possible to get opportunities for quiet intercourse with those who seemed interested. Filled with thankfulness for these and other advantages, he wrote home about the dress he had adopted, "It is evidently to be one's chief help for the interior."

And it was "the interior" more and more on which his heart was set. A few weeks in his new home at the South Gate brought wonderful soul-refreshing.

> Dr. Parker is in Ningpo [he wrote early in October] but I am not alone. I have such a sensible presence of God with me as I never before experienced, and such drawings to prayer and watchfulness as are very blessed and necessary.

Then, though a little place of his own was welcome and the opportunities around him were many, Hudson Taylor set out again for the "regions beyond." His Christian teacher was left to look after the interested neighbors in Shanghai and other missionaries were doing fine, intensive work in that great center. It might not seem so fruitful a method —to go as far afield as possible, scattering the Word of God—but it was following the Lord's teaching and example, and unless this course were adopted, *how should those farther on ever hear at all?*

Joy and sorrow strangely mingled in the days that followed, for he was prospered on this journey, yet the outcome brought him into trouble. The great island of Tsungming was his destination, with its population of more than a million without a single Protestant missionary. In company with Mr. Burdon, Hudson Taylor had visited Tsungming the year before, but now a very different reception awaited him. At his first landing place the people simply would not hear of his leaving. Dressed like themselves he did not seem a foreigner. His medicine chest attracted them no less than his preaching, and when they learned that he would need an upstairs room, because of the dampness of the locality, they said:

"Let him live in the temple, if no other upper story can be found."

But a householder was forthcoming whose premises included some sort of attic, and within three days of his arrival Hudson Taylor found himself in possession of his first home in "inland China."

This was wonderful, and so was the response to his message. Neighbors dropped in every day to the meetings and the stream of visitors and patients seemed unceasing. Six weeks of this happy work, while it wakened some opposition on the part of the medical fraternity, resulted in a group of earnest inquirers. One of these was a blacksmith named Chang, and another a businessman in good standing, "whose heart the Lord opened." His own first convert, Kwei-hwa, and another Christian helper were with him, so that when Hudson Taylor had to return to Shanghai for supplies the little group was still well cared for.

And then the disappointment came which was as painful as it was unexpected. Unknown to him, there had been some wirepulling at Tsungming. A high official had been induced by certain doctors and druggists to relieve them of the presence of one whom they considered their rival, though the young missionary accepted no payment for his medical work. A summons to the British Consulate awaited him, and his plea to be allowed to remain on the island, where all seemed peaceful and friendly, was in vain. The Consul reminded him that the British treaty only provided for residence in the Ports, and that if he attempted to settle elsewhere he rendered himself liable to a fine of five hundred dollars. He must give up his house, remove his belongings to Shanghai and be careful not to transgress in future, and that in spite of the fact that French priests were living on Tsungming, protected by a supplementary treaty which stipulated, as Hudson Taylor well knew, that immunities granted to other nations should also apply to the British. He might have appealed to a higher authority, but meanwhile could only accept the Consul's decision.

It was a heartbroken letter that he wrote home that evening. Those young inquirers—Chang, Sung and the others—what was to become of them? Were they not his own children in the faith? How could he leave them with no help and so little knowledge in the things of God? Yet the Lord had permitted it. The work was His. He would not fail them nor forsake them.

"My heart will be truly sorrowful when I can no longer join you in the meetings," said the blacksmith the last evening they were together.

"But you will worship in your own home," replied his friend. "Still shut your shop on Sunday, for God is here whether I am or not. Get someone to read for you, and gather your neighbors in to hear the Gospel."

"I know but very little," put in Sung, "and when I read I by no means understand all the characters.

My heart is grieved because you have to leave us; but I do thank God that He ever sent you to this place. My sins, once so heavy, are all laid on Jesus, and He daily gives me joy and peace."

Perplexed and disappointed, the young missionary could only wait upon God as to his future course.

Pray for me, pray for me [he wrote to his parents at this time]. I need more grace, and live far below my privileges. Oh, to feel more as . . . the Lord Jesus did when He said, "I lay down my life for the sheep." I do not want to be as a hireling who flees when the wolf is near, nor would I lightly run into danger when much may be accomplished in safety. I want to know the Lord's will and to have grace to do it, even if it results in expatriation. "Now is my soul troubled. and what shall I say? . . . Father, glorify thy name." Pray for me, that I may be a follower of Christ not in word only, but in deed and in truth.

All unknown to the troubled heart there was another, stronger, deeper than his own and more experienced in the things of God, that was facing the same problem. This man also was burdened for the perishing millions of inland China. He too had been testing the possibilities of itinerant evangelism and had found encouraging openings for such work. He had failed, however, in his effort to reach Nanking and was shut up to living on boats. slowly making his way back to the coast. William Burns, preacher and evangelist whom God had so signally used throughout Scotland and Canada in the mighty revival of 1839, was even then nearing Shanghai,

and there it was that he was brought into touch with
Hudson Taylor in his hour of need. It was not
long before each recognized a kindred spirit, in spite
of their disparity in years. Like Paul and Timothy
they drew together, and those wintry days saw the
commencement of a friendship destined to mold not
only Hudson Taylor's missionary life but the character of the far-reaching enterprise that was to develop under his guidance.

Not one boat but two now traveled in company
over the network of waterways leading inland from
Shanghai. Each missionary had a Chinese missionary with him as well as other helpers, and daily
worship on the boats grew into quite a little service.
Mr. Burns had developed a line of his own in such
work which his companion was glad to follow.
Choosing an important center, they might remain
two or three weeks in one place. Every morning
they set out early with a definite plan, sometimes
going together and sometimes separating to visit
different sections. Mr. Burns believed in beginning
quietly on the outskirts of any city in which foreigners had rarely been seen, and working his way
by degrees to the more crowded quarters. So they
would give some days to preaching in the suburbs,
gradually approaching the thronging streets and
markets, until they could pass anywhere without
endangering the shopkeepers' tempers or their wares.
Then they would visit temples, schools and tea shops,
returning regularly to the best places for preaching.
Announcing at each meeting when they would be

there again, they had the satisfaction of seeing the same faces frequently, and interested hearers could be invited to the boats for further conversation.

As time went on, Mr. Burns did not fail to notice that Hudson Taylor, though so much younger and less experienced, had the more attentive hearers and was even asked into private houses while he himself was requested to wait outside. The riffraff of the crowd always seemed to gather round the preacher in foreign dress, while those who wished to hear undisturbed followed his less noticeable friend. The result was a conclusion of which Mr. Burns tells in the following letter:

January 26, 1856

It is now forty-one days since I left Shanghai on this last occasion. An excellent young English missionary, Mr. Taylor of the Chinese Evangelization Society, has been my companion . . . and we have experienced much mercy, and on some occasions considerable help in our work.

I must once more tell the story I have had to tell more than once already, how four weeks ago, on the 29th of December, I put on Chinese dress which I am now wearing. Mr. Taylor had made this change a few months before, and I found that he was in consequence so much less incommoded in preaching, etc., by the crowd, that I concluded that it was my duty to follow his example. . . .

We have a large, very large field of labour in this region, though it might be difficult in the meantime for one to establish himself in any particular place. The people listen with attention, but we need the power from on high to convince and convert. Is there any spirit of prayer on our behalf among God's people in Kilsyth? Or is there any effort to seek this spirit? How great the need is, and how great the arguments and motives for prayer in this case! The harvest here is indeed great, and the labourers are few and imperfectly fitted, without much grace, for such a work. And yet, grace can make a few feeble instruments the means of accomplishing great things—things greater even than we can conceive.

Prayer was the atmosphere of William Burns's life and the Word of God was his daily food.

He was mighty in the Scriptures [his biographer records] and his greatest power in preaching was the way in which he used "the sword of the Spirit" upon men's consciences and hearts. . . . Sometimes one might have thought, in listening to his solemn appeals, that one was hearing a new chapter in the Bible when first spoken by a living prophet. . . . His whole life was literally a life of prayer, and his whole ministry a series of battles fought at the mercy-seat. . . . In digging in the field of the Word, he threw up now and then great nuggets which formed part of one's spiritual wealth ever after.

Cultured, genial and overflowing with mother-wit, he was an ideal companion. Sacred music was his delight. A wonderful fund of varied anecdotes gave charm to his society, and he was generous in recalling his experiences for the benefit of others. And this man, the friendship of this man, with all he was and had been, was the gift and blessing of God at this particular juncture to Hudson Taylor. Under its influence he grew and expanded and came to an understanding of spiritual values that left its impress on his whole after life. William Burns was better to him than a college course with all its advantages, because he lived out before him, right there in China, the reality of all he most needed to be and know.

For seven long happy months they worked together, first in the Shanghai region, then in and around the great city of Swatow. The call to this southern port had come most unexpectedly, and they had the privilege of being the first missionaries in that difficult but now fruitful field. But for their Chinese dress it would have been impossible to live right in the native city as they did, and to make friends of so many of their turbulent neighbors. At the end of four months they were able, through the blessing of God upon the medical work, to rent the entire premises in which they had been allowed but a single room, and their initial difficulties seemed at an end.

Then it was that at Mr. Burns's request his young companion consented to return to Shanghai, to obtain his medical outfit left there for safety. As though the shadow of a longer parting lay upon his heart, Hudson Taylor was reluctant to take the step. To leave Mr. Burns alone to face the worst heat of summer was no less distressing than to break up the companionship which had meant so much in his life.

Those happy months were an unspeakable joy
and comfort to me [he recalled long after]. Never
had I such a spiritual father as Mr. Burns; never
had I known such holy, happy intercourse. His
love for the Word was delightful, and his holy
reverential life and constant communings with God
made fellowship with him to satisfy the deep
cravings of my heart.

But the instruments and medicines were needed,
for Mr. Burns was keen about developing hospital
work. So Hudson Taylor sailed for Shanghai, only
to find that his medical supplies had all been acci-
dentally destroyed by fire. And before he could
replace them, the distressing news reached him that
his beloved and honored friend had been arrested
by the Chinese authorities and sent, under escort,
a journey of thirty-one days to Canton. The shock
was all the more painful as they were forbidden to
return to Swatow, and the path that had seemed so
clear before them was lost in strange uncertainty.

Yet but for this great and unexpected trial Hudson Taylor might never have been led into the life-
work that was awaiting him; might never have
known the love beyond all other human love which
was to be his crowning joy and blessing.

7

GOD'S WAY—"PERFECT"

We thank Thee, Lord, for pilgrim days
When desert springs were dry,
When first we knew what depths of need
Thy love could satisfy.

—SELECTED

OVER THE POLITICAL HORIZON, storm clouds had long been gathering, and the very mail that brought tidings of the arrest of Mr. Burns told also of the outbreak of hostilities between England and China. It was at Ningpo that Hudson Taylor heard of the bombardment of Canton by the British fleet, and the commencement of the war which did not finally terminate until four years later. His first thought, naturally, was for Mr. Burns. What a mercy that he was no longer at Swatow, exposed to the rage of that hotheaded southern people!

As you are aware [he wrote to his sister in November] I have been detained in Ningpo by various circumstances, and a sufficient cause has at

77

length appeared in the disturbances which have broken out in the South. The latest news we now have is that Canton has been bombarded for two days, a breach being made on the second, and that the British entered the city, the Viceroy refusing to give any satisfaction. We are anxiously awaiting later and fuller accounts. . . . I know not the merits of the present course of action . . . and therefore refrain from writing my thoughts about it. But I would just refer to the goodness of God in removing Mr. Burns from Swatow *in time*. For if one may judge the feelings of the Cantonese in Swatow by what one sees here at present, it would go hard with any one at their mercy.

So, already, the circumstance that had seemed a great calamity was being recognized as among the "all things" that work together for good "to them that love God." It was one of not a few hard lessons through which Hudson Taylor was learning to think of God as The One Great Circumstance of Life, and of *all* lesser, external circumstances as necessarily the kindest, wisest, best, because either ordered or permitted by Him. And it was not long before he came to see in his detention in Ningpo another remarkable evidence of the love and care of God. For it was there he was brought into contact with the life that was so perfectly to complete his own.

In the southern section of the city, near the ancient pagoda, was a quiet street between two lakes which went by the name of Bridge Street. There Dr. Parker had opened a dispensary, a mile or two from his hospital, and there as autumn was advancing Hudson Taylor was glad to find a temporary home. The little place is of interest, as later on it was to be the first station of the China Inland Mission—working now from hundreds of centers throughout many provinces. Looking back upon those early days, Mr. Taylor wrote:

I have a distinct remembrance of tracing my initials on the snow which during the night had collected on my coverlet in the large, barnlike upper room now divided into four or five smaller ones, each of which is comfortably ceiled. The tiling of a Chinese house may keep off the rain, if it happens to be sound, but does not afford so good protection against snow, which will beat up through the crannies and crevices and find its way within. But however unfinished may have been its fittings, the little house was well adapted for work among the people, and there I thankfully settled, finding ample scope for service, morning, noon and night.

The only other foreigners in that part of the city were Mr. and Mrs. J. Jones, also of the Chinese Evangelization Society, and a lady who with two young helpers was carrying on a remarkably successful school for girls, the first ever opened in China. This Miss Aldersey was fortunate in having secured the assistance of the daughters of the Rev. Samuel Dyer, who had been one of the earliest missionaries to the Chinese and a colleague of Robert Morrison's. When Mr. and Mrs. Jones and their family came to live not far from the school, the younger of the

sisters found many opportunities of being helpful
to the busy mother. As often as possible they went
out visiting in the neighborhood, Miss Dyer's flu-
ency in the language making such work a pleasure.
Young as she was, not yet twenty, and much occupied with her school duties, this bright, gifted
girl was a real soul-winner. With her, missionary
work was not teaching merely, it was definitely
leading people to Christ.

This was what drew out Hudson Taylor's interest.
For in the home of his fellow workers he could not
but meet Miss Dyer from time to time, and could
not but be attracted. She was so frank and natural
that they were soon good friends, and she proved
so like-minded in all important ways that unconsciously almost to himself she began to fill a place
in his heart never filled before.

But before long the friendship was interrupted by
unexpected happenings which broke up the missionary community in Ningpo. A plot was discovered to massacre all foreigners, and though
thwarted in their design, the hatred of the Cantonese throughout the district was so great that it
seemed necessary to send families with children to
the coast. His familiarity with the Shanghai dialect
made Hudson Taylor the most suitable escort for
the party, and hard though it was to leave at such
a time he could not refuse the service.

Miss Aldersey was not to be persuaded to seek a
place of greater safety. On account of advancing
age, she was handing over her school to the Amer-

ican Presbyterian Mission. It was no time for unnecessary changes, and taking what precautions were
possible she encouraged her young helpers to remain with her. The elder of the sisters had become engaged to Hudson Taylor's special friend,
Mr. J. S. Burdon, and the younger seemed the more
lonely and unprotected by comparison. How hard
it was to leave her at such a time! But Hudson
Taylor had no reason to suppose that his presence
would be any comfort. And besides—was he not
trying to forget?

For one thing, he realized keenly how little he
had to offer the one he loved. His position as an
agent of the Chinese Evangelization Society had of
late become increasingly embarrassing. For some
time he had known that the Society was in debt
and that his salary was paid from borrowed money.

Personally [he wrote, recalling the circumstances]
I had always avoided debt, though at times only
by very careful economy. Now there was no difficulty in doing this, for my income was larger,
but the Society itself was in debt. The quarterly
bills which I and others were instructed to draw
were often met with borrowed money, and a correspondence commenced which terminated in the
following year by my resigning from conscientious
motives.

To me it seemed that the teaching of God's Word
was unmistakably clear: "Owe no man anything."
To borrow money implied to my mind a con-
tradiction of Scripture—a confession that God had
withheld some good thing, and a determination

to get for ourselves what He had not given. Could
that which was wrong for one Christian be right
for an association of Christians? Or could any
amount of precedents make a wrong course justi-
fiable? If the Word taught me anything, it taught
me to have no connection with debt. I could not
think that God was poor, that He was short of
resources, or unwilling to supply any want of whatever work was really His. It seemed to me that if
there were lack of funds to carry on work, then to
that degree, in that special development, or at that
time, it could not be the work of God. To satisfy
my conscience I was therefore compelled to resign
my connection with the Society. . . . It was a great
satisfaction to me that my friend and colleague,
Mr. Jones, . . . was led to take the same step, and
we were both profoundly thankful that the separation took place without the least breach of friendly feeling on either side. . . .

The step we had taken was not a little trying to
faith. I was not at all sure what God would have
me do or whether He would so meet my need as
to enable me to continue working as before. . . .
But God blessed and prospered me, and how glad
and thankful I felt when the separation was really
effected! I could look right up into my Father's
face with a satisfied heart, ready by His grace to
do the next thing as He might teach me, and feeling very sure of His loving care.

And how blessedly He did lead me I can never,
never tell. It was like a continuation of some of
my earlier experiences at home. My faith was not
untried; it often, often failed, and I was so sorry

and ashamed of the failure to trust such a Father.
But oh! I was learning to know Him. I would not
even then have missed the trial. He became so
near, so real, so intimate! The occasional difficulty
about funds never came from an insufficient supply
for personal needs, but in consequence of ministering to the wants of scores of the hungry and dying
around us. And trials far more searching in other
ways quite eclipsed these difficulties and being
deeper brought forth in consequence richer fruits.

The poor whom they were feeding that winter
were famine refugees who had crowded to Shanghai
from districts devastated by the Taiping Rebellion.
In all stages of nakedness, sickness and starvation,
these sufferers were living in low, arched tombs
which they had broken open, or in any discarded
building half in ruins. In addition to taking charge
of one of the chapels of the London Mission, Hudson Taylor was preaching daily in the City Temple,
but he made time to visit these haunts of misery
with Mr. Jones, ministering regularly to the sick
and feeding many of the hungry.

Thus it was from no lack of occupation that his
thoughts turned constantly to Ningpo, nor was it
without misgiving that he found himself so urgently impelled to consider the question of marriage.
"Never marry if you can help it" is cryptic advice
which may easily be misunderstood, but Hudson
Taylor was finding out its meaning. For a great,
God-given love had come to him, and there was no
disguising its implications.

Meanwhile, in Ningpo, the same gracious Providence was working, though there was much more in the way of hindrance to overcome. The difficulty, however, was not on the part of the one most concerned. Maria Dyer's was a deep and tender nature. Lonely from childhood, she had grown up longing for a real heart-friend. Her father she could hardly remember, and her mother had died when she was only ten years old. Her true conversion, when on the way to China to join Miss Aldersey, made missionary work very different from what it would otherwise have been, but it was a lonely post for a girl still in her teens, especially after her sister became engaged to be married.

And then, he had come—the young missionary who impressed her as having longings like her own after holiness, usefulness, nearness to God. He was different from others—not more gifted or attractive, though he was bright and pleasing and full of quiet fun, but with a something about him that made her feel rested and understood. He seemed to live in such a real world and to have such a real, great God. Though she saw but little of him it was a comfort to know that he was near, and she was startled to find how much she missed him when after only seven weeks he left to return to Swatow.

And then the way was closed, as we have seen, and to her joy as well as surprise, he was back in Ningpo again. Perhaps it was this that opened her eyes to the feeling with which she was beginning to regard him. At any rate she soon knew and with

her sweet true nature did not try to hide it from
her own heart and God. There was no one else to
whom she cared to speak about him, for others did
not always see in him what she saw. They disliked
his wearing Chinese dress, and did not approve of
his making himself so entirely one with the people.
His Chinese dress—how she loved it! or what it
represented, rather, of his spirit. His poverty and
generous giving to the destitute — how well she
understood, how much she sympathized! Did others
think him visionary in his longing to reach the great
beyond of untouched need? Why, that was just the
burden on her heart, the life she too would live,
only for a woman it seemed if anything more im-
practicable. So she prayed much about her friend,
though to him she showed but little.

Month after month went by, when he had to be
in Shanghai, and she did not know it cost him anything to leave her. And then, at last—a letter! Sud-
den as was the joy, the great and wonderful joy,
it was no surprise, only a quiet outshining of what
had long shone within. So she was not mistaken
after all. They *were* for one another—"two whom
God hath chosen to walk together before Him."

When she could break away from her first glad
thanksgiving she went to find her sister, who was
most sympathetic. The next thing was to tell Miss
Aldersey, hoping she would approve this engagement as she had Burella's. But great was the indignation with which the older lady heard the story.

"Mr. Taylor! that young, poor, unconnected Nobody. How dare he presume to think of such a thing? Of course the proposal must be refused at once, and that finally."

In vain Maria tried to explain how much he was to her. That only made matters worse. She must be saved without delay from such folly. And her kind friend, with the best intentions, proceeded to take the matter entirely into her own hands. The result was a letter written almost at Miss Aldersey's dictation, not only closing the whole affair but requesting most decidedly that it might never be reopened.

Bewildered and heartbroken, the poor girl had no choice. She was too young and inexperienced, and far too shy in such matters, to withstand the decision of Miss Aldersey, strongly reinforced by others of her friends. Stung to the quick with grief and shame, she could only leave it in the hands of her heavenly Father. He knew, He understood. And in the long, lonely days that followed, even when her sister was won over to Miss Aldersey's position, she took refuge in the certainty that nothing, *nothing* was too hard for the Lord. "If He has to slay my Isaac," she assured herself again and again, "I know He can restore."

But when spring came again and the absentees were able to return from Shanghai, the position became increasingly difficult. For Miss Aldersey, indignant at Hudson Taylor's reappearance, felt it her duty to disparage him in every possible way. He could not attempt to see Miss Dyer, after the

letter she had written, and had no clue to her
changed attitude. Gifted and attractive, she had no
lack of suitors who were openly encouraged. And
Chinese etiquette combined with well-meant diplo-
macy made it almost impossible for the two to meet.
But both were praying. Both hearts so sorely tried
were open to God, truly desiring His will. And
He has wonderful ways of working!

It was a sultry afternoon in July, and in regular
rotation it had come to Mrs. Jones's turn to be
hostess for the prayer meeting. The usual number
of ladies gathered, but as the sequel proved it was
easier to come to the meeting that day than to get
away. For with scarcely any warning a water-
spout, sweeping up the tidal river, broke over
Ningpo in a perfect deluge followed by torrents of
rain. Mr. Jones and Hudson Taylor, by this time
a boarder in their family, were over at the dispensary, and on account of the flooded streets were late
in returning. Most of the visitors had left before
they reached home, but a servant from the school
was there who said that Miss Maria Dyer and a companion were still waiting for sedan chairs.

"Go into my study," said Mr. Jones, "and I will
see what can be arranged."

It was not long before he returned, saying that
the ladies were alone with Mrs. Jones, and would
be glad to see Mr. Taylor.

Hardly knowing what he did, the young man
went upstairs and found himself meeting the one he
supremely loved. True there were others present—

that was unavoidable on account of Chinese conventions. But he hardly saw them, hardly saw anything but her face. He had only meant to ask if he might write to her guardian in London—for permission. But now it all came out, he could not help it! And she? Well, there were only intimate friends with them, and it might be so long before they could meet again! Yes, she consented, and did much more than that. With a true woman's heart, she relieved his fears by letting him understand that he was just as dear to her as she could be to him. And then Hudson Taylor relieved the situation by saying, "Let us take it all to the Lord in prayer."

Four months was a long, long time to wait, especially when they knew that Miss Aldersey had written home to bring the distant relatives to her own point of view. What if the guardian in London should be influenced by her strong representations? What if he refused his consent to the marriage? Both the young people were clear in their convictions that the blessing of God rested upon obedience to parents, or those in parental authority.

I have never known [Mr. Taylor wrote in later years] disobedience to the definite command of a parent, even if that parent were mistaken, that was not followed by retribution. Conquer through the Lord. He can open any door.[1] The responsibility

---

[1] Mr. Taylor was then dealing specially with the question of a call to missionary work, the consent of one or both parents being withheld.

is with the parent in such a case, and it is a serious
one. When the son or daughter can say in all sincerity, "I am waiting for Thee, Lord, to open the
way," the matter is in His hands and He will take
it up.

And take it up His did; for toward the end of
November the long-looked-for letters came, and
were favorable! After careful inquiry, the uncle
in London had satisfied himself that Hudson Taylor was a missionary of unusual promise. The secretaries of the Chinese Evangelization Society had
nothing but good to say of him, and from other
sources also he had the highest references. Taking, therefore, any disquieting rumors he may have
heard for no more than they were worth, he cordially consented to his niece's engagement, requesting
only that the marriage should be delayed until she
came of age. And that would be in little more than
two months' time.

After that they were openly engaged, and how
those happy winter days made up for all that had
gone before! On Saturday, January 16, the bride-
elect would be twenty-one years of age, and the wed-
ding was arranged for the week following.

I never felt in better health or spirits in my life
[wrote Hudson Taylor]. . . . I can scarcely realize,
dear Mother, what has happened; that after all the
agony and suspense we have suffered we are not
only at liberty to meet and be much with each
other, but that within a few days, D.V., we are to
be married! God *has* been good to us. He has

indeed answered our prayer and taken our part against the mighty. Oh, may we walk more closely with Him and serve Him more faithfully. I wish you knew my Precious One. She is such a treasure! She is all that I desire.

And then, six weeks later:

Oh, to be married to the one you *do* love, and love most tenderly and devotedly . . . that is bliss beyond the power of words to express or imagination conceive. There is no disappointment *there*. And every day as it shows more of the mind of your Beloved, when you have such a treasure as mine, makes you only more proud, more happy, more humbly thankful to the Giver of all good for this best of earthly gifts.

8

JOY OF HARVEST

Sheaves after sowing, sun after rain,
Sight after mystery, peace after pain.

—F. R. Havergal

ONLY TWO AND A HALF YEARS remained of
Hudson Taylor's first period of service in China,
but they were rich, full years. The little house on
Bridge Street was now home indeed. Downstairs,
the chapel and guest hall remained the same, and
the Christians and inquirers came and went freely,
but upstairs one could hardly recognize the barnlike
attic in the cheery little rooms whose curtained windows looked out on the narrow street in front and
the canal behind. And what a difference it made
that the women and children could be cared for
equally with the men! Mrs. Taylor, already well
known in the neighborhood, was now more than
ever welcome as she went visiting, and since "all
the world loves a lover" the attraction of those
united hearts was widely felt.

One of their warmest friends and helpers was the

ex-Buddhist leader, who was a cotton merchant in the city. This Mr. Ni, though long resident in Ningpo, had never come in contact with the Gospel. He was deeply earnest, and as president of an idolatrous society spent much time and money in the service of "the gods." But his heart was not at rest, and the more he followed his round of religious observances the more empty he found them to be.

Passing an open door on the street one evening, he noticed that something was going on. A bell was being rung and people were assembling as if for a meeting. Learning that it was a hall for the discussion of religious matters he too went in, for there was nothing about which he was more concerned than the penalties due to sin and the transmigration of the soul on its unknown way. A young foreigner in Chinese dress was preaching from his Sacred Classics. He was at home in the Ningpo dialect and Mr. Ni could understand every word of the passage he read. But what could be its meaning?

> As Moses lifted up the serpent in the wilderness, even so must the Son of man be lifted up. . . . For God so loved the world, that he gave his only begotten Son, that whosoever believeth in him should not perish, but have everlasting life. For God sent not his Son into the world to condemn the world; but that the world through him might be saved.

Saved, not condemned; a way to find everlasting life; a God who *loved* the world; a serpent, no, a

"Son of man" lifted up—what could it all be about? To say that Ni was interested scarcely begins to express what went on in his mind. The story of the brazen serpent in the wilderness, illustrating the divine remedy for sin and its deadly consequences; the life, death and resurrection of the Lord Jesus Christ; the bearing of all this upon his own needs, brought home to him in the power of the Spirit— well, it is the miracle of the ages, and thank God, we see it still! "I, if I be lifted up, will draw all men unto me."

But the meeting was coming to a close. The foreign teacher had ceased speaking. With the instinct of one accustomed to lead in such matters, Ni rose in his place, and looking round on the audience said with simple directness:

"I have long sought the Truth, but without finding it. I have traveled far and near, but have never searched it out. In Confucianism, Buddhism, Taoism, I have found no rest. But I do find rest in what we have heard tonight. Henceforth, I am a believer in Jesus."

He became an ardent student of the Bible and his growth in knowledge and grace was wonderful. Not long after his conversion, he obtained permission to address a meeting of the society over which he had formerly presided, and Mr. Taylor who accompanied him was deeply impressed by the clearness and fullness with which he set forth the Gospel. One of his former followers was led to Christ through his testimony, and Ni began to know the joy of the soulwinner.

He it was who, talking with his missionary friend, unexpectedly raised the question: "How long have you had the Glad Tidings in your country?"

"Some hundreds of years," was the reluctant reply.

"What! hundreds of years?"

"My father sought the Truth," he continued sadly, "and died without finding it. Oh, why did you not come sooner?"

It was a moment, the pain of which Hudson Taylor could never forget, and which deepened his earnestness in seeking to bring Christ to those who might still be reached.

Great was the need of patience, in those days, not to run before the Spirit of God in the matter of engaging full-time helpers in the work. For as yet the young missionaries had no regular Chinese associates. Mr. Ni was eagerly devoting all the time he could spare from his business, and so were Neng-kuei the basket-maker, Wang the farmer of Hosi, and Tsiu the teacher with his warmhearted mother. But they and others were all occupied in their necessary avocations through the day, though they drew to the mission house in the evening and spent much time there on Sundays. It would have been easy to employ the Christian teacher in the school to which Mrs. Taylor was giving many hours daily, or to take on others at a modest salary to train them for positions of usefulness. But this, the missionaries realized, would have proved a hindrance in the long run rather than a help. To pay young converts, however sincere, for making known the Gospel—and to pay them with money from foreign sources—must inevitably weaken their influence if not their Christian character. The time might come when their call of God to such work would be evident to all, and when the Christians themselves would be ready to support them. How was China ever to be evangelized but by the Chinese Church? And how were the converts ever to know the joy of unpaid, voluntary service, from love to the Lord Jesus Christ, unless the missionaries could be patient and wait for spiritual developments?

So it was a full life that Hudson Taylor and his colleagues led, while the young converts were growing up around them. For he was doing not a little medical work in addition to preaching on the streets and in the chapel, receiving visitors, attending to correspondence and accounts, and keeping up evangelistic excursions. But nothing was allowed to interfere with the main business in hand—that of daily helpful intercourse with the Christians and inquirers.

Little wonder, with such love and care lavished upon them, that the converts grew in grace and in knowledge of the things of God. Evening by evening the missionaries would be at their disposal, and after the regular public meeting, three periods were given to carefully prepared study. To begin with, a lesson was taken from the Old Testament, when Hudson Taylor delighted to unfold its spiritual teaching. Then, after an interval, a chapter was read in *Pilgrim's Progress* or some other helpful book. And finally a passage from the New Testament was talked over and applied to practical life. This was the regular order every night, leading up to Sunday with its special services for worship and for reaching outsiders.

And Sunday had its teaching periods too. It cost the Christians not a little to close shop and store, sacrificing as far as their business affairs were concerned one day in seven. Yet Hudson Taylor and his colleagues knew that no strong, self-propagating church can be built up on any other basis. They determined therefore to do their utmost to make the sacrifice worthwhile, by filling the hours thus given to God with helpful and joyous occupation. Between the regular services, Christians, inquirers, patients, schoolchildren and servants were divided into classes and taught in a bright, personal way. This made Sunday a heavy day for the missionaries, for there were only four of them; but if it cost some toil and weariness, they were the better able to appreciate the sacrifices made by the converts. Some had to walk long distances and go without food the greater part of the day, and others had to face persecution and personal loss. But they were willing, most of them, for all it involved, if only they could have the Lord's day for worship, for they were conscious of the difference it made all through the week.

So the church was growing and the missionaries were developing, and opportunities for service were enlarging before them. The Treaty of Tientsin, signed in the summer after Hudson Taylor's marriage, had opened the way at last to all the inland provinces. Foreigners had now the right to travel freely, under the protection of passports, and it only remained to make use of the facilities for which they had prayed so long.

You will have heard before this all about the new treaty [Mr. Taylor wrote in November]. We may be losing some of our Ningpo missionaries . . . who will go inland. And oh, will not the Church at home awaken and send us out many more to publish the Glad Tidings?

Many of us long to go—oh, how we long to go! But there are duties and ties that bind us that none but the Lord can unloose. May He give "gifts" to many of the native Christians, qualifying them . . . for the care of churches already formed, . . . and thus set us free for pioneering work.

This was the burden on their hearts—to raise up, by the blessing of God, a church that should be self propagating as well as self-supporting—and the claim of the little band of believers who still needed them as parents in the Lord could not be set aside. It was to their love, their prayers, these souls had been committed, and to leave them now, even for the good of others, would have been to disregard the highest of all trusts, parental responsibility. And they were right in this conviction, as the sequel abundantly proved.

For these Christians, Ni, Neng-kuei, Wang and the rest, were men whom God could use. Poor and unlearned as most of them were, they too were to become "fishers of men." No fewer than six or seven of these early converts were to come to the help of their beloved leader in the formative years of the China Inland Mission. But for their co-operation, the new project, humanly speaking, could never have been realized. It would be difficult to overestimate all that grew out of the intensive work at Bridge Street at this time. For what the missionaries were themselves, this to a large extent their children in the faith became, and there is no better, surer way of passing on spiritual blessing.

In the midst of all this joy of harvest, a great and unexpected sorrow called Hudson Taylor to new responsibilities. Over in the Settlement, Dr. Parker had recently completed his new hospital. Splendidly situated near one of the city gates and overlooking the river, its commodious buildings attracted the notice of thousands daily. Everything about the place was admirably adapted to the needs of the work built up through patient years. But in the doctor's home were stricken hearts, for the brave man who had overcome so many difficulties was mourning the loss of his wife, who after only a few hours' illness had passed away, leaving four young children. One of them was seriously ill, and the doctor realized that he must take them home to Scotland. But what about the hospital? The wards were full of patients and the dispensary was crowded

day by day with a stream of people needing help.
No other doctor was free to take his place, and yet
to close down with the winter coming on seemed
unthinkable. Though there were no funds to leave
for the work—for it was supported from the pro-
ceeds of his private practice—perhaps his former colleague, Hudson Taylor, could carry on the dispensary at any rate. So the unexpected proposition
was put before him.

After waiting upon the Lord for guidance [Mr.
Taylor recalled] I felt constrained to undertake not
only the dispensary but the hospital as well, relying solely on the faithfulness of a prayer-hearing
God to furnish means for its support.

At times there were no fewer than fifty in-
patients, besides a large number who attended the
dispensary. Thirty beds were ordinarily allotted
to free patients and their attendants, and about as
many more to opium smokers who paid their board
while being cured of the habit. As all the wants
of the sick in the wards were supplied gratuitously,
as well as the medical supplies needed for the out-
patient department, the daily expenses were considerable. Hospital attendants also were required,
involving their support. The funds for the main-
tenance of all this had hitherto been supplied by
the doctor's foreign practice, and with his departure this source of income ceased. But had not God
said that whatever we ask in the name of the Lord
Jesus shall be done? And are we not told to seek
first the kingdom of God—not means to advance it—
and that "all these things" shall be added to us?
Such promises were surely sufficient.

It did not matter to the young missionaries that the situation was unlooked-for; that none of their friends at home could have foreseen it; and that months must go by before there could be any response to letters. Were not they themselves looking to the Lord only for support, and had He ever failed them? The secret of faith that is ready for emergencies is the quiet, practical dependence upon God day by day which makes Him real to the believing heart.

Eight days before entering upon the care of the Ningpo hospital [wrote Mr. Taylor] I had not the remotest idea of ever doing so; still less could friends at home have foreseen the need.

But the Lord had anticipated it, as events were fully to prove.

When the assistants left by Dr. Parker learned of the changed conditions, and that there were only funds in hand for the expenses of the current month, after which prayer would be the only resource, they not unnaturally decided to withdraw and open the way for other workers. It was a change Dr. Parker had long desired to make, only he had not known how to obtain helpers of a different sort. Hudson Taylor did know, and with a lightened heart he turned to the little circle that did not fail him. For to the Bridge Street Christians it seemed quite as natural to trust the Lord for temporal blessings as for spiritual. Did not the greater include the less; and was He not, as their "teacher" so often reminded them, a *real* Father, who never could forget His children's needs? So to the hospital they came, glad not only to strengthen the hands of their missionary friends but to prove afresh to themselves and all concerned the faithfulness of God. Some worked in one way and some in another; some giving what time they could spare, and others giving their whole time without promise of wages, though receiving their support. And all took the hospital and its concerns on their hearts in prayer.

No wonder a new atmosphere began to permeate dispensary and wards. Account for it the patients could not—at any rate at first—but they enjoyed none the less the happy, homelike feeling, and the zest with which everything was carried on. The days were full of a new interest. For these attendants— Wang the grass-cutter and Wang the painter, Ni, Neng-kuei and others—seemed to possess the secret of perpetual happiness, and had so much to impart. Not only were they kind and considerate in the work of the wards, but all their spare time was given to telling of One who had transformed life for them and who, they said, was ready to receive all who came to Him for rest. Then there were books, pictures and singing. Everything indeed seemed set to song! And the daily meetings in the chapel only made one long for more.

There are few secrets in China, and the financial basis upon which the hospital was now run was not one of them. Soon the patients knew all about it, and were watching eagerly for the outcome. This too was something to think and talk about; and as the money left by Dr. Parker was used up and Hudson Taylor's own supplies ran low, many were the conjectures as to what would happen next. Needless to say that alone and with his little band of helpers Hudson Taylor was much in prayer at this time. It was perhaps a more open and in that sense more crucial test than any that had come to him, and he realized that the faith of not a few was at stake as well as the continuance of the hospital work. But day after day went by without bringing the expected answer.

At length one morning Kuei-hua the cook[1] appeared with serious news for his master. The very last bag of rice had been opened, and was disappearing rapidly.

"Then," replied Hudson Taylor, "the Lord's time for helping us must be close at hand."

And so it proved. For before that bag of rice was finished a letter reached the young missionary that was among the most remarkable he ever received.

It was from Mr. Berger, and contained a check for fifty pounds, like others that had come before. Only in this case the letter went on to say that a heavy burden had come upon the writer, the burden of wealth to use for God. Mr. Berger's father had recently passed away, leaving him a considerable increase of fortune. The son did not wish to enlarge his personal expenditure. He had had

---

[1] This was the same valued servant who had been with Mr. Taylor in Shanghai, Tsungming and elsewhere and who was now a bright Christian.

enough before and was now praying to be guided
as to the Lord's purpose in what had taken place.
Could his friends in China help him? The draft
enclosed was for immediate needs, and would they
write fully, after praying over the matter, if there
were ways in which they could profitably use more.

Fifty pounds! There it lay on the table; and his
far-off friend, knowing nothing about that last bag
of rice or the many needs of the hospital, actually
asked if he might send them more. No wonder
Hudson Taylor was overwhelmed with thankfulness
and awe. Suppose he had held back from taking
charge of the hospital on account of lack of means,
or lack of faith rather? Lack of faith—with such
promises and such a God!

There was no Salvation Army in those days, but
the praise meeting held in the chapel fairly anticipated it in its songs and shouts of joy. But unlike
some Army meetings it had to be a short one, for
were there not the patients in the wards? And how
they listened—those men and women who had known
nothing all their lives but blank, empty heathenism.

"Where is the idol that can do anything like
that?" was the question upon many lips and hearts.
"Have they ever delivered us in our troubles, or
answered prayer after this sort?"

9

HIDDEN YEARS

Oh, to save these! to perish for their saving;
Die for their life; be offered for them all.

—Selected

BUT IT TOLD, this busy, happy work, upon those who were engaged in it. Within nine months, sixteen patients from the hospital had been baptized, while more than thirty others were candidates for admission to one or other of the Ningpo churches. But six years in China, six such years, had left their mark, and Hudson Taylor's strength was failing rapidly.

People are perishing, and God is so blessing the work [he wrote to his father]. But we are wearing down and must have help. . . .

Do you know of any earnest, devoted young men desirous of serving God in China, who, not wishing for more than their actual support, would be willing to come out and labour here? Oh, for four or five such helpers! They would probably begin to preach in Chinese in six months' time, and in answer to prayer the means for their support would be found.

"People are perishing and God is so blessing the work"—it was the urgency of these facts that carried Hudson Taylor through serious illness and the painful parting, when he was invalided home in 1860. It was the urgency of these facts that sustained him through the years that followed, when it seemed as though the doctors were right in thinking that he would never be strong enough to return to China. The great need, as he had seen it, and a deep sense of responsibility burned as a steady fire in his soul, and neither poor health, lack of encouragement nor any other difficulty could lessen his sense of call to bring Christ to those perishing millions.

Settling in the east end of London, to be near his old hospital, Mr. Taylor was able as health improved to resume his medical studies. He also undertook the task of revising the romanized Ningpo Testament, the Bible Society having agreed to publish a new edition. And for a time there was a good deal of correspondence with young men who were considering China as a field for life service, which resulted in the going out of one, one only, to join Mr. and Mrs. Jones in Ningpo.[1] But gradually outside interest seemed to lessen, and Mr. and Mrs. Taylor found themselves, with few friends, shut up to prayer and patience. At twenty-nine and twenty-four years of age it was not easy to be

---

[1]Mr. James Meadows sailed for China in 1862, three years before the inauguration of the China Inland Mission, of which he was for more than fifty years an honored member. Two of his daughters are still in China, members of the Mission.

set aside, cut off from the work they loved and left
in the backwater of that dreary street in a poor part
of London. Yet, without those hidden years with
all their growth and testing, how could the vision
and enthusiasm of youth have been matured for the
leadership that was to be?

Five long, hidden years — and we should have
known little of their experiences but for the discovery in an old, dusty packing-case, of a number
of notebooks, small and thin, filled with Mr. Taylor's handwriting. One after another we came upon them among much useless rubbish, until the
complete series lay before us—twelve in number, not
one missing. And what a tale was unfolded as, often
blinded with tears, one traced the faded record!

For these unstudied pages reveal a growing in-
timacy with God and dependence upon Him. Faith
is here, and faithfulness down to the smallest detail.
Devotion is here and self-sacrifice, leading to unremitting labor. Prayer is here, patient persevering prayer, wonderfully answered. But there is something more: there is the deep, prolonged exercise
of a soul that is following hard after God. There
is the gradual strengthening here, of a man called
to walk by faith not by sight; the unutterable confidence of a heart cleaving to God and God alone,
which pleases Him as nothing else can.

"Without faith it is impossible to please [or sat-
isfy] him: for he that cometh to God must believe
that he is, and that he is a rewarder of them that
diligently seek him."

Outwardly the days were filled with quiet, ordinary duties, enriched with trials and joys of many kinds. The little daughter who had brought such happiness in Ningpo had now three younger brothers. Home and children had to be cared for with very limited means, and faith was often tested as Mr. and Mrs. Taylor went on in the pathway of direct dependence upon God. The work in Ningpo had also to be provided for and directed, which involved a good deal of correspondence. The New Testament revision was a task that seemed to grow rather than diminish, as it had come to include the preparation of marginal references. These proved of great value to the Ningpo Christians, and the labor of preparing them, while it was considerable, brought no little blessing to the young missionary who was spending hours every day over the Word of God.

The amount of work he was enabled to get through is amazing, and could hardly be credited but for this record. Every day Mr. Taylor noted the time given to his main task, and one frequently comes upon entries such as the following:

April 27, Revision seven hours (evening at Exeter Hall).
April 28, Revision nine and a half hours.
April 29, Revision eleven hours.
April 30, Revision five and a half hours (Baptist Missionary Society meetings).
May 1, Revision eight and a half hours (visitors till 10 P. M.).

May   2, Revision thirteen hours.

May   3, Sunday at Bayswater: In the morning
          heard Mr. Lewis, from John 3:33; took
          the Communion there in the afternoon.[1]
          Evening, stayed at home and engaged in
          prayer about our Chinese work.

May   4, Revision four hours (correspondence and
          visitors) .

May   5, Revision eleven and a half hours.

May   6, Revision seven hours   (important inter-
          views) .

May   7, Revision nine and a half hours.

May   8, Revision ten and a half hours.

May   9, Revision thirteen hours.

May 10, Sunday: Morning, with Lae-djun on
Heb. 11, first part, a happy season.[2] Wrote to
James Meadows.   Afternoon, prayer with Maria
about leaving this house, about Meadows, True-
love, revision, etc. Wrote to Mr. Lord.[3] Evening,
heard Mr. Kennedy on Matt. 27:42—"He saved
others, himself he cannot save."   Oh, to be more

---

[1]Bayswater in the west end of London, was at this time
the home of Mr. Taylor's sister Amelia, recently married to
Mr. B. Broomhall. The Rev. W. G. Lewis was the minister
of the Baptist church of which Mr. Taylor had become a
member.

[2]Lae-djun was one of the Ningpo Christians who had vol-
unteered to come to England, without salary, to help Mr. and
Mrs. Taylor in their work. This association had not a little
to do with his subsequent usefulness as the first and for
thirty years one of the most devoted pastors in the China
Inland Mission.

[3]The Rev. E. C. Lord of Ningpo, though connected with
the American Baptist Mission, found time to replace Mr. J.
Jones in the care of the Bridge Street Church, and to give
much help to Mr. and Mrs. Meadows. Mr. Jones had been
obliged to leave China on account of illness, and did not live
to reach England.

like the meek, forbearing, loving Jesus! Lord,
make me more like Thee.

The meetings referred to were a large part of
Mr. Taylor's work at this time, for he was doing
his utmost to induce the denominational boards to
take up the evangelization of inland China. Alone
or with his colleague in the revision, the Rev. F. F.
Gough of the C.M.S., he visited the secretaries of
various societies, putting before them the need of
that long-neglected field, made accessible by the
granting of passports for travel and even residence
in the interior. But, while everywhere meeting with
a sympathetic hearing, it became evident that none
of the boards was prepared to assume responsibility
for so great an undertaking.

All this, naturally, reacted in one way on Hudson
Taylor, and when to his personal knowledge of certain parts of China was added a careful study of the
whole field, the result was overwhelming. For he
had been requested by his friend and pastor, Mr.
Lewis, editor of the *Baptist Magazine,* to write a
series of articles to awaken interest in the Ningpo
Mission. These he had begun to prepare and one
had already been published when Mr. Lewis returned the manuscript of the second. The articles
were too important and weighty, he felt, to be restricted to a denominational paper.

"Add to them," he urged, "let them cover the
whole field and be published as an appeal for inland China."

This led to detailed study of the spiritual needs

of every part of China, and of its outlying dependencies. While in Ningpo, the pressure of claims immediately around him had been so great that Mr. Taylor had been unable to give much thought to the still greater needs further afield. But now—daily facing the map on the wall of his study and the open Bible whose promises were gripping his soul—he was as near the vast provinces of inland China as the places in which he had labored near the coast. Little wonder that "prayer was the only way by which the burdened heart could obtain any relief"!

But the real crisis came when prayer no longer brought relief, but seemed to commit him more and more to the undertaking from which he shrank. For he began to see in the light of that open Book that God could use him, even him, to answer his own prayers.

I had a growing conviction [he wrote] that God would have *me* seek from Him the needed workers and go forth with them. But for a long time unbelief hindered my taking the first step. . . .

In the study of that divine Word, I learned that to obtain successful workers, not elaborate appeals for help, but first earnest prayer to God to thrust forth labourers, and second the deepening of the spiritual life of the Church, so that men should be unable to stay at home, were what was needed. I saw that the apostolic plan was not to raise ways and means, but to go and do the work, trusting His sure promise who has said, "Seek ye first the kingdom of God and his righteousness, and all these things shall be added unto you." . . .

But how inconsistent unbelief always is! I had no doubt but that if I prayed for fellow-workers, in the name of the Lord Jesus Christ, they would be given. I had no doubt but that, in answer to such prayer, the means for our going forth would be provided, and that doors would be opened before us in unreached parts of the Empire. But I had not then learned to trust God for keeping power and grace for myself, so no wonder I could not trust Him to keep others who might be prepared to go with me. I feared that amid the dangers, difficulties and trials necessarily connected with such work, some comparatively inexperienced Christians might break down, and bitterly reproach me for encouraging them to undertake an enterprise for which they were unequal.

Yet what was I to do? The sense of bloodguiltiness became more and more intense. Simply because I refused to ask for them, the labourers did not come forward, did not go out to China: and every day tens of thousands in that land were passing into Christless graves! Perishing China so filled my heart and mind that there was no rest by day and little sleep by night, till health gave way.

For the hidden years had done their work. An instrument was ready that God could use, and the prevailing prayers going up from that little home in East London were to receive a speedy though unexpected answer.

10

A MAN SHUT UP TO GOD

Nothing before, nothing behind:
    The steps of faith
Fall on the seeming void, and find
    The rock beneath.

J. G. WHITTIER

SUMMER HAD COME again, and the streets were hot and dusty in East London. Seeing that Mr. Taylor was not looking well, an old friend invited him down to the coast to spend a few days at Brighton. Mrs. Taylor, who was concerned about his health, was glad to see him go, though she understood only in part the experiences through which he was passing. Even to her, he could not fully show the exercise of soul that was becoming unbearable.

So it was alone on the sands at Brighton that Sunday morning, that he met the crisis of his life. He had gone to church with others, but the sight of multitudes rejoicing in the blessings of salvation was more than he could bear. "Other sheep I have" —the lost and perishing in China, for whose souls

no man cared—"them also I must bring." And the
tones of the Master's voice, the love in the Master's
face pleaded silently.

He knew that God was speaking. He knew, as
we have seen, that if he yielded to His will, and
prayed under His guidance, evangelists for inland
China would be given. As to their support, he had
no anxiety. He who called and sent them would
not fail to give them daily bread. But what if *they*
should fail? For Hudson Taylor was facing no
unknown situation. He was familiar with conditions in China, the real temptations to be met, the
real enemy entrenched on his own ground. What if
fellow workers were overborne and laid the blame
on him?

> It was just a bringing in of self through unbelief;
> the devil getting one to feel [he recalled] that
> while prayer and faith would bring one into the
> fix, one would have to get out of it as best one
> might. And I did not see that the power that
> would give the men and the means would be suf-
> ficient to keep them also, even in the far interior
> of China.

Meanwhile, a million a month were dying in that
great, waiting land—dying without God. This was
burned into his soul. A decision had to be made
and he knew it, for the conflict could no longer be
endured. It was comparatively easy to pray for
workers, but would he, could he accept the burden
of leadership?

> In great spiritual agony, I wandered out on the

sands alone. And there the Lord conquered my
unbelief, and I surrendered myself to God for this
service. I told Him that all the responsibility as
to the issues and consequences must rest with Him;
that as His servant it was mine to obey and to follow Him, His to direct, care for and guide me and
those who might labour with me. Need I say that
at once peace flowed into my burdened heart?

Then and there I asked Him for twenty-four fellow-workers, two for each of the eleven provinces
which were without a missionary and two for
Mongolia; and writing the petition on the margin
of the Bible I had with me, I turned homeward
with a heart enjoying rest such as it had been a
stranger to for months, and with an assurance that
the Lord would bless His own work and that I
should share in the blessing. . . .

The conflict ended, all was peace and joy. I
felt as if I could fly up the hill to Mr. Pearce's
house. And how I did sleep that night! My dear
wife thought that Brighton had done wonders for
me, and so it had.

11

A MAN SENT FROM GOD

Thou on the Lord rely,
  So safe shalt thou go on;
Fix on His work thy stedfast eye,
  So shall thy work be done.

PAUL GERHARDT

HAPPY THE MAN, called to go forward in any pathway of faith, who has in his life-companion only sympathy and help. For seven and a half years —perfect years as concerned their married life— Hudson Taylor had known no disappointment in the one he loved, and she did not fail him now. Frail in health and only twenty-eight years of age, Mrs. Taylor's hands were full with the care of four young children, yet from the moment she learned of her husband's call to the great, the seemingly impossible, task of the evangelization of inland China she became in a new way his comfort and inspiration. Her hand wrote for him, her faith strengthened his own, her prayers undergirded the whole work and her practical experience and loving heart made her the Mother of the Mission.

For very soon the larger house at Coborn Street into which they had moved began to fill up with candidates for China. The parlors that had seemed so spacious could scarcely accommodate the friends who gathered for the Saturday prayer meeting. The fifty dollars (all he had) with which Mr. Taylor had opened a bank account in the name of "The China Inland Mission" grew into hundreds, through the voluntary, unasked gifts of those who desired to have part in the work; and plans began to form themselves for the outgoing of the first party.

Picture then the sitting room at Number 30 Coborn Street on Sunday—the only day when Mr. Taylor could find time for quiet writing. At the table Mrs. Taylor is seated, pen in hand, while he paces to and fro, absorbed in the subject on their hearts. For the articles Mr. Lewis suggested have taken on new meaning. There is not only an urgent need to make known, but a new departure, a definite effort to meet that need in dependence upon God. *China's Spiritual Need and Claims* was the pamphlet that came into being as they prayed and wrote, wrote and prayed; and perhaps no book of modern times proved more effective in moving the hearts of the people of God. How many it sent to China as edition after edition was published, how many it drew into sympathy with missionary work the wide world over, how it strengthened faith and quickened prayer and devotion will never be known until the secrets of all hearts are revealed. "Every

sentence was steeped in prayer," and every sentence
seemed to live with the power of God.

The book made many friends and many openings.
It had to be reprinted within three weeks of pub-
lication, and drew forth letters such as the following from the late Lord Radstock:

> I have read your pamphlet and have been great-
> ly stirred by it. I trust you may be enabled by the
> Holy Spirit to speak words which will thrust forth
> many labourers into the vineyards Dear Brother,
> enlarge your desires! Ask for a hundred labourers,
> and the Lord will give them to you.[1]

Not a hundred, however, but just twenty-four was
the first objective, and a well-worn Bible lies before
us now in which that prayer is recorded in Mr.
Taylor's clear though faded writing. Far from being elated at the turn events were taking, success
only added to his sense of responsibility, and it was
a man burdened with a God-given message who
moved from place to place that memorable winter,
awakening other hearts to a like God-consciousness.

For it seemed a new thing, in those days, to talk
about *faith* as a sufficient financial basis for missionary undertakings at the other end of the world.
"Faith missions" were unheard of, the only organizations then in existence being the regular denominational boards. But Hudson Taylor, young though
he was, had learned to know God in a very real

---

[1] This startling though prophetic suggestion was accompanied by a generous gift of $500. Lord Radstock lived to see
the time when Mr. Taylor did ask for a hundred workers
in one year, and when in answer to prayer they were given.

way. He had seen Him, as he wrote, quell the raging of a storm at sea, in answer to definite prayer, alter the direction of the wind, and give rain in a time of drought. He had seen Him, in answer to prayer, stay the hand of would-be murderers and quell the violence of enraged men. He had seen Him rebuke sickness in answer to prayer, and raise up the dying, when all hope of recovery seemed gone.[2] For more than eight years he had proved His faithfulness in supplying the needs of his family and work in answer to prayer, unforeseen as many of those needs had been. How could he but encourage others to put their trust in the love that cannot forget, the faithfulness that cannot fail?

We have to do with One [he reminded his hearers] who is Lord of all power and might, whose arm is not shortened that it cannot save, nor His ear heavy that it cannot hear; with One whose unchanging Word directs us to ask and receive that our joy may be full, to open our mouths wide, that He may fill them. And we do well to remember that this gracious God, who has condescended to place His almighty power at the command of believing prayer looks not lightly on the bloodguiltiness of those who neglect to avail themselves of it for the benefit of the perishing. . . .

To those who have never been called to prove the faithfulness of the covenant-keeping God . . . it might seem a hazardous experiment to send

²Details of these experiences will be found in the first volume of Mr. Taylor's larger biography, especially pages 429-492. See *Hudson Taylor in Early Years: The Growth of a Soul*, by the present writers.

twenty-four European evangelists to a distant heathen land "with only God to look to"; but in one whose privilege it has been, through many years, to put that God to the test—at home and abroad, by land and sea, in sickness and in health, in dangers, necessities, and at the gates of death— such apprehensions would be wholly inexcusable.

The work they were undertaking was far too great to be limited to any one denomination. The fact that the Mission offered no salaries was in itself enough to deter all but those whose experience made them sure of God, and such souls possess a union in more than name.

We had to consider [Mr. Taylor continued] whether it would not be possible for members of various denominations to work together on simple, evangelistic lines, without friction as to conscientious differences of opinion. Prayerfully concluding that it would, we decided to invite the co-operation of fellow-believers, irrespective of denominational views, who fully held the inspiration of God's Word and were willing to prove their faith by going to inland China with only the guarantee they carried in their Bibles.

That Word said, "Seek ye first the kingdom of God and his righteousness, and all these things [food and raiment] shall be added unto you." If anyone did not believe that God spoke the truth, it would be better for him not to go to China to propagate the faith; if he did believe it, surely the promise sufficed. Again, we have the assurance, "No good thing will he withhold from them that walk uprightly." If anyone did not mean to walk uprightly, he had better stay at home; if he did mean to walk uprightly, he had all he needed in the shape of a guarantee fund. God owns all the gold and silver in the world, and the cattle on a thousand hills. We need not be vegetarians!

We might indeed have had a guarantee fund if we had wished it; but we felt that it was unnecessary and would do harm. Money wrongly placed and money given from wrong motives are both greatly to be dreaded. We can afford to have as little as the Lord chooses to give, but we cannot afford to have unconsecrated money, or to have money placed in the wrong position. Far better have no money, even to buy bread with. There are plenty of ravens in China, and the Lord could send them again with bread and flesh. . . . He sustained three million Israelites in the wilderness for forty years. We do not expect Him to send three million missionaries to China, but if He did He would have ample means to sustain them all.

Let us see that we keep God before our eyes; that we walk in His ways and seek to please and glorify Him in everything, great and small. Depend upon it, God's work, done in God's way, will never lack God's supplies.

One thing greatly concerned Mr. Taylor, and that was that the new enterprise should not deflect men or means from previously existing agencies. Robbing Peter to pay Paul, in this sense, would be no advantage to the work of God. To open the way for workers who might not be accepted by other missions, whose preparation had not included university training, was part of the plan, and no one was to be asked to join the Inland Mission. If the Lord of the harvest wanted them in that particular field, He would put it into their hearts to offer. In the same way, there were to be no appeals for money. If the Mission could be sustained in answer to prayer, without subscription lists or solicitation of any kind for funds, it might grow up among the older societies without danger of diverting gifts from their accustomed channels. It might even be helpful, by directing attention to the Great Worker, and affording a practical illustration of its underlying principle that God, God *alone*, is sufficient for God's own work.

For the rest, they were content with little in the way of organization. It was wonderful how provision was made for the home side of the work. In Mr. and Mrs. Berger of Saint Hill, friends had been raised up who bore it upon their hearts almost as did Mr. and Mrs. Taylor. They prayed for it and lived for it with equal devotion, turning their beautiful home into a center for all the interests of the Mission.

> When I decided to go forward [Mr. Taylor said of this relationship], Mr. Berger undertook to represent us at home. The thing grew up gradually. We were much drawn together. The Mission received its name in his drawing room. Neither of us asked or appointed the other—it just *was so*.

Essential spiritual principles were talked over with the candidates and clearly understood as the

basis of the Mission. A few simple arrangements
were agreed to in writing, in Mr. Berger's presence,
that was all.

We came out as God's children at God's command [was Mr. Taylor's simple statement] to do
God's work, depending on Him for supplies; to
wear native dress and to go inland. I was to be
the leader in China. . . There was no question as
to who was to determine points at issue.

In the same way, Mr. Berger was responsible at
home. He would correspond with candidates, receive and forward contributions, publish an *Occasional Paper* with audited accounts, send out suitable reinforcements as funds permitted and keep
clear of debt. This last was a cardinal principle
with all concerned.[3]

It is really just as easy [as Mr. Taylor pointed
out] for God to give *beforehand,* and He much
prefers to do so. He is too wise to allow His purposes to be frustrated for lack of a little money;
but money obtained in unspiritual ways is sure to
hinder blessing.

There were problems, many of them, that only
experience could solve, and Mr. Berger's practical
illustration often came to mind. He was a man of
affairs, a manufacturer of starch, at the head of a
prosperous business. He knew that like the trees
on his estate, a live thing will grow.

[3]From the first it was made perfectly clear that Mr. Taylor
never drew for himself or his family upon the funds of the
Mission. He had the joy, however, as the Lord enabled him,
of contributing largely to its support. "As poor, yet making
many rich."

You must wait for a tree to grow [he said in this connection] before there can be much in the way of branches. First you have only a slender stem, with a few leaves or shoots. Then little twigs appear. Ultimately, these may become great limbs, all but separate trees. But it takes time and patience. If there is life, it will develop after its own order.

The many answers to prayer, as the first party of the Mission made their preparations for sailing, cannot be dwelt upon now. Wonderful indeed they were! so much so that an inset had to be put into the first *Occasional Paper* saying that the whole sum referred to as needed for passage and outfits was already in hand. But behind these experiences lay the noon hour of prayer every day in Mr. Taylor's home, as well as the weekly gathering there and at Saint Hill and special days for prayer and fasting. It all meant a very close and happy walk with God.

Human nothingness, divine sufficiency—the one just as real as the other—was the atmosphere of those last days at Coborn Street. Friends could not come and go without feeling it. Among packing-cases and bundles, the last prayer meetings were held, people crowding the rooms and staircase, sitting on anything that came to hand. On the wall still hung the map; on the table lay the open Bible.

Our great desire and aim [Mr. Taylor had written of the new mission] are to plant the standard of the Cross in the eleven provinces of China hitherto unoccupied, and in Chinese Tartary.

"A foolhardy business," said those who saw only the difficulties.

"A superhuman task," sighed others who wished them well. And many even of their friends could not but be anxious.

"You will be forgotten," was the concern of some. "With no committee or organization before the public, you will be lost sight of in that distant land. Claims are many nowadays. Before long you may find yourselves without even the necessaries of life!"

"I am taking my children with me," was the quiet answer, "and I notice it is not difficult to remember that they need breakfast in the morning, dinner at midday and supper at night. Indeed, I could not forget them if I tried. And I find it impossible to think that our heavenly Father is less tender and mindful of His children than I, a poor earthly father, am of mine. No, He will not forget us!"

And through all the years since then, with all they have brought, that confidence has been amply justified.

12

SPIRITUAL URGENCY

Men die in darkness at your side,
  Without a hope to cheer the tomb;
Take up the torch and wave it wide,
  The torch that lights time's thickest gloom.

—H. BONAR

THAT THERE WAS a sustaining power behind
the leaders and many of the first workers of the
new mission is very manifest from the records of
the next few years. One cannot but be impressed
by the urgency of spirit that characterized them—
a great, twofold urgency that carried them through
every kind of difficulty and trial. There was the
urgency of love to the Lord Jesus Christ that made
them glory in their privilege of knowing Him in
the fellowship of His sufferings in a new and deeper
way, and there was in them the urgency of His
constraining love for the souls of the perishing by
whom they were surrounded. It may seem old-
fashioned in these days to talk of souls, perishing
souls, needing salvation. But the theology of John
3:16 is a motive power that accomplishes results in

and through believers that all the wisdom and resources of the world cannot equal.

God so loved . . . that he gave his only begotten Son, that whosoever believeth in him should not *perish,* but have everlasting life.

We may have more wealth in these days, better education, greater comfort in traveling and in our surroundings even as missionaries, but have we the spirit of urgency, the deep, inward convictions that moved those who went before us; have we the same passion of love, personal love for the Lord Jesus Christ? If these are lacking, it is a loss for which nothing can compensate.

* * * * *

Over the dark blue sea, over the trackless flood,
A little band is gone in the service of their God;
   The lonely waste of waters they traverse to proclaim
   In the distant land of Sinim, Immanuel's saving Name.
They have heard from the far-off East the voice of their brothers' blood:
A million a month in China are dying without God.

No help have they but God: alone to their Father's hand
They look for the supply of their wants in a distant land.
   The fulness of the world is His; "all power" in earth and heaven;
   They are strong tho' weak and rich tho' poor, in the promise He has given.

'Tis enough! they hear the cry, the voice of their
　　brothers' blood:
A million a month in China are dying without
　　God.[1]

* * * * *

Four months' voyage on a sailing ship of less than
eight hundred tons' burden was no small undertaking, with a party of sixteen missionaries and four
young children. But much prayer had been made
beforehand, not only for safety by the way but for
a crew to whom God would bless His Word. One
day was given to getting things in order in their
cabins, and then Chinese study commenced, Mr.
Taylor taking a class in the morning and Mrs.
Taylor one in the afternoon. There were times
when all the students were down with seasickness,
and the teachers had to do duty as steward and
stewardess. But they were good sailors, and the
younger people soon found their sea legs. How
young they all were! their leader at thirty-four being much the senior of the party.

At close quarters on that little sailing ship character was tested, and it was easy for the crew to see
how far these passengers lived up to their profession.
Needless to say they were keenly watched, at work
and in their hours of relaxation. Doing all they
could to make the voyage pleasant for the ship's company, the missionaries prayed and waited. Then the
sailors themselves asked for meetings, and a work

---

[1]From verses by the Rev. H. Grattan Guinness, on the
sailing of the first party of the China Inland Mission, May
26, 1866.

of God began which resulted in the conversion of a large majority of the crew. It is a wonderful record, as one reads it in letters written at the time, and makes it very evident that the pioneers of the Mission were living for nothing less than to win souls to Christ. They were not faultless, and one reads of failures that hindered blessing. But these were not taken as a matter of course. They were deplored and confessed with a sincerity which restored fellowship in the Lord.

Then, unable to wreck the usefulness of the party, it seemed as though the great adversary, "the prince of the power of the air," determined to send them, ship and all, to the bottom. It was nothing short of a miracle that they ever reached their destination, for all the way up the China Sea they were hardpressed by storm and tempest. For fifteen days the stress of one typhoon after another was upon them, until they were almost a wreck.

The appearance of things was now truly terrific [Mr. Taylor wrote after twelve days of this experience] . . . Rolling fearfully, the masts and yards hanging down were tearing our only sail . . . and battering like a ram against the mainyard. The deck from forecastle to poop was one scarcely broken sea. The roar of the water, the clanging of chains, the beating of the dangling masts and yards, the sharp smack of the torn sails made it almost impossible to hear any orders that might be given.

And for three days after that the danger only in-

creased, as the ship was making water fast. Fires
were all out and cooking was impossible. For a
time no drinking water was obtainable, and the
women as well as the men worked at the pumps.
But through it all prayer was so wonderfully answered that no lives were lost or serious injuries
sustained. Kept in the peace which passes understanding, even the mother anxious for her children
was enabled, as she wrote, "to enter into Habakkuk's
experience as never before—'Yet I will rejoice in the
Lord, I will joy in the God of my salvation.'"

No less wonderful were the answers to prayer a
little later when the party set out from Shanghai,
all in Chinese dress, to seek a home inland. Traveling by houseboats, the ladies and children could be
sheltered from curious crowds as city after city was
passed, while efforts were being made to find premises in which some of the young men might settle.
But only disappointment awaited them. Again and
again when it seemed they had succeeded, negotiations fell through and they had to move on, an
unbroken party, toward Hangchow. Two or three
missionary families had already taken up residence
in that city, and it would have meant serious risk
to them as well as to the new arrivals if the coming
of so large a party stirred up opposition. Yet, what
were they to do? Autumn was far advanced and
the nights on the water were bitterly cold. Several
of the party were more or less ill and the boat people were clamoring to go home for the winter. Never
had Mr. Taylor realized his responsibilities more

than when he left the boats in a quiet place outside the city and went ahead to seek the accommodation so urgently needed.

Mrs. Taylor was feeling the situation no less keenly, as with quiet, confident faith she gathered the younger missionaries for prayer, telling them of the comfort that had come to her through the Psalm in her regular reading that morning: "Who will bring me into the strong city? who will lead me into Edom? Wilt not thou, O God? . . . Give us help from trouble; for vain is the help of man." Together they read it now, and the prayer that followed changed an hour of painful suspense into one of fellowship long to be remembered.

Could it be Mr. Taylor's voice that stirred the boat-people outside? Could he be back so soon? And what tidings did he bring? "Before they call, I will answer; and while they are yet speaking, I will hear." Yes, all was well! A home was ready, waiting for them. One of the Hangchow missionaries was absent for a week and had left word that his house, comfortably furnished, was at the disposal of Mr. Taylor's party. Situated on a quiet street, it could be reached in the boats without observation, and that very night the weary, thankful travelers were at rest in the great city.

And within the next few days, in spite of all the usual difficulties, Mr. Taylor was enabled to secure premises of their own—a large rambling house which had once been a mandarin's residence, but in course of time had become a regular rabbit warren, oc-

cupied by a number of families. It lent itself well
to adaptation, and while the new owners were only
in part possession they were able to begin missionary work within their own doors, without attracting
too much attention. It does not need many words
for a loving heart to overflow, and Miss Faulding,
the youngest of the party, was already able to make
herself understood by the women.

We have been getting the house a little more
comfortable [she wrote in the middle of Decem-
ber] though there is plenty still to be done. Mr.
Taylor and the young men have contrived paper
ceilings fixed on wooden frames, which keep out
some of the cold air—for the upstairs rooms have
roofs such as you find in chapels at home. They
also have papered some of the partitions between
the rooms. Of course we are as yet in confusion,
but we are getting on, and I hope shall be settled
some day.

The lodgers are to leave next week. They occupy
principally the ground floor. . . . I am so glad for
them to have been here, for many have come to
Chinese prayers and listened attentively. We could
not have visited out of doors yet, . . . but I read
and talked with those women every day and they
seem to like it. One woman I have great hope of.

Before Christmas there were attentive audiences
of fifty or sixty at the Sunday services, and Mr. Taylor had made at least one evangelistic journey. In
the neighboring city of Siaoshan he and Mr. Meadows had found excellent opportunities for preaching the Gospel and had been enabled to rent a

small house, with a view to settling out some of the
new arrivals as soon as possible. His letters to Mr.
Berger show the spirit in which they were facing
their great task.

> You will be glad to learn that facilities for send-
> ing letters by native post and for transmitting
> money . . . to the interior are very good. I do not
> think there will be any difficulty in remitting
> money to any province in the empire which will
> not be easily overcome. In the same way, letters
> from the most distant parts can be sent to the ports.
> Such communication is slow and may prove rather
> expensive, but it is tolerably sure. Thus we see
> the way opening before us for work in the interior.

> It is pretty cold weather [Dec. 4] to be living in
> a house without any ceilings and with very few
> walls and windows. There is a deficiency in the
> wall of my own bedroom six feet by nine, closed
> in with a sheet, so that ventilation is decidedly
> free. But we heed these things very little. Around
> us are poor, dark heathen—large cities without any
> missionary, populous towns without any mission-
> ary, villages without number, all without the means
> of grace. I do not envy the state of mind that
> would forget these, or leave them to perish, for
> fear of a little discomfort. May God make us
> faithful to Him and to our work.

Meanwhile his hands were more than full in
Hangchow. With the Chinese New Year, patients
crowded to the dispensary, as many as two hundred
in a day, and an equal number attended the Sunday services. When the first reinforcements arrived

from home, early in 1867, Mr. Taylor was too busy
to see anything of them until hours later. He was
standing on a table at the time, preaching to a
crowd of patients in the courtyard, and could only
call out a hearty welcome as the party entered, escorted by Mr. Meadows. The new arrivals were
more than satisfied with this state of affairs, and it
was not long before John McCarthy was at Mr.
Taylor's side, soon to become his chief helper in
the medical work. Those were days when, amid
external hardships, his fellow workers had the opportunity of at any rate close association with the
leader they loved, who embodied to so large an
extent their ideals.

> I think of him as I ever knew him [Mr. McCarthy
> wrote from western China thirty-eight years later],
> kind, loving, thoughtful of everyone but himself, a
> blessing wherever he went and a strength and com-
> fort to all with whom he came in contact . . . a
> constant example of all that a missionary ought
> to be.

Yet there were some, even in those early days
who, through failure in their own spiritual life, became critical of all around them. The spirit that
had caused trouble on the voyage was still in evidence, and Mrs. Taylor suffered no less than her
husband through the aspersions made. Not until
months later, however, did she mention the matter,
even in writing to Mrs. Berger, so anxious were
they to conquer the trouble by love and patience.

It was in answer to inquiries from Saint Hill that she wrote at length:

> Do pray for us very much, for we do so need God's preserving grace at the present time. We have come to fight Satan in his very strongholds, and he will not let us alone. What folly were ours, were we here in our own strength! But greater is He that is for us than all that are against us. . . . I should be very sorry to see discord sown among the sisters of our party, and this is one of the evils I am fearing now. . . . What turn the N—— matter will take I cannot think. One thing I know: "the hope of Israel" will not forsake us. One is almost tempted to ask, "Why was N—— permitted to come out?" Perhaps it was that our Mission might be thoroughly established on right bases early in its history.

Sorrows of another kind were permitted to test faith and endurance as the summer wore on, but all the while souls were being saved and the church built up which numbers over fifteen hundred members today. When the first baptisms came in May, Mrs. Taylor wrote again to Mrs. Berger:

> Perhaps the dear Lord sees that we need sorrows to keep us from being elated at the rich blessing He is giving in our work.

But she little anticipated the overwhelming personal sorrow the hot season was to bring.

Sweetest and brightest of all their children was the little daughter given them in Ningpo, who by this time was almost eight years old. Full of love to the Lord Jesus and to the people around them,

she was no little help in the work as well as with
her younger brothers, to whom she was all a sister
could be. But with the long hot days Gracie began
to droop, and though the children were taken to the
hills nothing could save the little life.

Beside his dying child in the old, ruined temple,
Mr. Taylor faced the situation for himself and
those he loved best.

It was no vain nor unintelligent act [he wrote to
Mr. Berger] when, knowing this land, its people
and climate, I laid my wife and children with myself on the altar for this service. And He whom so
unworthily, yet in simplicity and godly sincerity,
we are and have been seeking to serve—and with
some measure of success—He has not left us now.

To his mother, Mr. Taylor wrote more freely.

Our dear little Gracie! How we miss her sweet
voice in the morning, one of the first sounds to
greet us when we woke, and through the day and
at eventide! As I take the walks I used to take with
her tripping figure at my side, the thought comes
anew like a throb of agony, "Is it possible that I
shall nevermore feel the pressure of that little
hand . . . nevermore see the sparkle of those bright
eyes?" And yet she is not lost. I would not have
her back again. I am thankful she was taken
rather than any of the others, though she was the
sunshine of our lives. . .

I think I never saw anything so perfect, so beautiful as the remains of that dear child. The long,
silken eyelashes under the finely arched brows; the
nose, so delicately chiseled; the mouth, small and

sweetly expressive; the purity of the white features
. . . all are deeply impressed on heart and memory.
Then her sweet little Chinese jacket, and the little
hands folded on her bosom, holding a single flow-
er—oh, it was passing fair, and so hard to close
forever from our sight!

Pray for us. At times I seem almost overwhelmed
with the internal and external trials connected with
our work. But He has said, "I will never leave
thee, nor forsake thee," and "My strength is made
perfect in weakness." So be it.

In the sorrow of this bereavement Mr. and Mrs.
Taylor consecrated themselves afresh to the task of
reaching inland China with the Gospel. Before the
close of the year all the prefectural cities in Chekiang
had been visited. Nanking in the neighboring
province had been occupied, and the members of the
Mission were working in centers as much as twenty-
four days' journey apart. The church also in Hangchow was well established with Wang Lae-djun as
its pastor,[2] and as spring came again it was possible
for the leaders of the Mission to be spared from
that center.

Those were days when scarcely a station in China
was opened without danger to life itself. Riots were
so usual that they seemed almost part of the pro-
ceedings, and it was natural for Mr. Taylor to say
to a candidate who had lost a limb and could only
walk with the help of a crutch,

---

[2]Wang Lae-djun was the Ningpo friend who had accompanied Mr. and Mrs. Taylor to England.

"But what would you do in China if a riot broke out and you had to run away?"

"I had not considered running away," was the quiet answer. "I thought that 'the lame' were to 'take the prey.'"

And this he did, in actual fact, when the time came and he had the privilege of living down the troubles through which the Gospel came to Wenchow.

"Why don't you run away?" yelled the rioters who were robbing him of everything and had taken even his crutches.

"Run away!" he replied with a smile. "How can a man run with only one leg, I should like to know!"

Disarmed by his courage and friendliness, the better element prevailed, and the unseen power of prayer won the day.[3]

In the same spirit George Duncan, the tall, quiet Highlander, made his way in Nanking as the first resident missionary. Content to live in the Drum Tower, when he could get no other lodging, he shared an open loft with the rats and the deep-toned bell, spending his days amid the crowds in street and tea shop. When his supply of money was running low, his Chinese cook and only companion came to ask what they should do—as to

---

[3]It was shortly after the death of little Gracie that Mr. George Stott, who had already been some years in China, planted in the city and prefecture of Wenchow the church which now numbers (including all communicants) eight thousand adult members.

leave the city and the little place they had rented
would probably mean no possibility of return.

"Do?" said the missionary. "Why, we shall 'trust
in the Lord, and do good.' So shall we 'dwell in
the land' and verily we shall be fed."

Days went on, and Mr. Taylor found himself unable to reach Nanking by native banks. Finally, in
his anxiety for Duncan, he sent a brother-mission-
ary to relieve the situation. By this time the cook's
savings, willingly given to the work, were all used
up, and between them they had not a dollar left.
But Duncan had gone out to his preaching as usual,
saying to his anxious companion:

"Let us just 'trust in the Lord and do good.' His
promise is still the same, 'So shalt thou dwell in
the land, and verily *thou shalt be fed.*' "

That evening Rudland understood why the water
in the Grand Canal had run so low that he had been
obliged to finish his journey overland, for it brought
him to Nanking several days earlier than would
have been possible by boat. When he reached the
house it was to find cupboard and purse alike empty. Tramping the endless streets, Duncan had
preached all day and was returning tired and hungry
when, to his surprise, he saw his Chinese helper
running to meet him.

"Oh, sir," he cried breathlessly, "it's all right! It's
all right! Mr. Rudland—the money—a good supper!"

"Did I not tell you this morning," Duncan replied, laying a kindly hand on his shoulder, "that it is *always* 'all right' to trust in the living God?"

But Mr. Taylor was not content with getting the young men out into pioneering work. There were no dangers or hardships which he and Mrs. Taylor themselves were not ready to face, and the inward, spiritual urge was at least as strong in their hearts as in others in the Mission. It was not easy to leave Hangchow after sixteen months of settled life and work. The church already numbered fifty baptized believers, and many of the inquirers were full of promise. But with Wang Lae-djun as pastor, assisted by Mr. McCarthy, and with Miss Faulding caring for the women the good work would go on. There were lonely pioneers needing help, and teeming cities, towns and villages entirely without the Word of Life. Though it meant breaking up their home and taking the children to live on boats for a time, they set out in the spring, as we have seen, ready to join Duncan at Nanking, or to stay in any place that might open to them *en route.*

It was in the great city of Yangchow the travelers were enabled to settle after two months of boat life. They had spent three weeks with Mr. Henry Cordon, a member of the Mission who was just commencing work in the far-famed city of Soochow, and had come on to Chinkiang at the junction of the Grand Canal with the mighty Yangtze. Impressed with the strategic importance of this place, Mr. Taylor was soon in treaty for premises which they subsequently obtained, and finding that the negotia-

tions were likely to be prolonged they continued
their journey across the Yangtze and a few miles up
the northern section of the Grand Canal. Thus the
famous city of which Marco Polo had once been
governor was reached, its turreted walls enclosing a
population of three hundred and sixty thousand,
without any witness for Christ.

Were it not that you yourselves are old travellers [Mrs. Taylor wrote to Mrs. Berger] I should
think it impossible for you to realize our feelings
last Monday week, when we exchanged the discomfort of a boat into every room of which the
heavy rain had been leaking, for a suite of apart-
ments in a first-rate Chinese hotel—such a place as
my husband, who has seen a good deal of Chinese
travellers' accommodations, never before met with
—and that hotel, too, inside the city of Yangchow.

A friendly innkeeper and crowds of interested
visitors promised well at the beginning, and after
a favorable proclamation from the governor had appeared, a house was obtained into which the family moved in the middle of July. The heat was already trying, and they were hoping for quieter days
in August, but the rush of patients and visitors continued. The attraction of a foreign family in the
city was considerable, especially as Mr. Taylor
proved to be a skillful physician. Mrs. Taylor's
pleasing Chinese speech and manners attracted the
women, and just as in Hangchow, hearts seemed
opening to the Gospel.

But the enemy was busy. It could not be that

such an advance into his territory should be un-
challenged. The *literati* of the city held a meeting
and decided to stir up trouble. Anonymous hand-
bills appeared all over the city, attributing the most
revolting crimes to foreigners, especially those whose
business it was to propagate "the religion of Jesus."
Before long the missionaries realized that a change
was coming over the attitude of the people. Friendly visitors gave place to crowds of the lowest rab-
ble about the door, and a fresh set of posters added
fuel to the flame. By patience and kindliness rioting was averted again and again—Mr. Taylor hardly
daring to leave the entrance to the premises for
several days, where he was answering questions and
keeping the crowds in order.

Great was the thankfulness of the household,
augmented by the arrival of the Rudlands and Mr.
Duncan, when the storm seemed to have spent itself. The intense heat of August was broken by
torrential rains which effectually scattered the
crowds. But the relief was short-lived. Two foreigners from Chinkiang, wearing not the Chinese
dress adopted by the missionaries, but undisguised
foreign clothing, came up to visit Yangchow and
caused no little sensation. This was too good a
chance to be lost. The *literati* were again busy,
and no sooner had the visitors left with the impression that all was quiet, than reports began to
be circulated that children were missing in all directions. Twenty-four at least, so the people believed, had fallen a prey to the inhuman foreigners.

"Courage—avenge our wrongs!   Attack!   Destroy!
Much loot shall be ours!"

*   *   *   *   *

Forty-eight hours later, in a boat nearing Chinkiang, wounded, suffering but undismayed, the missionary party were thanking God for His marvelous
protection in the storm of murderous passions that
had almost overwhelmed them.

> Our God has brought us through [Mrs. Taylor
> wrote as they traveled], may it be to live hence-
> forth more fully to His praise and glory. We have
> had another typhoon, so to speak, not as prolonged
> as the literal one, nearly two years ago, but at least
> equally dangerous to our lives and more terrible
> while it lasted. I believe God will bring His own
> glory out of this experience, and I hope it will tend
> to the furtherance of the Gospel. . . .
>
> Yours in a present Saviour . . .

"A present Saviour"—how little could the rioters
have understood the secret of such calmness and
strength! Awed by something, they knew not what,
the raging mob had been restrained from the worst
deeds of violence. Death, though imminent, had
been averted again and again, and both Mr. Taylor,
exposed to all the fury of the crowds on his way to
seek the help of local authorities, and those he had
had to leave, who faced the perils of attack and fire
in their besieged dwelling, were alike protected by
the Unseen Hand.

But they were hours of anguish—anguish for the
mother as she sheltered the children and women of

the party in an upper room, from which they were driven at last by fire; anguish for the father, detained at a distance, hearing from the mandarin's *yamen* the yells of the rioters bent on destruction. Outwardly as calm as if there were no danger, Mrs. Taylor faced those terrible scenes, more than once saving life by her presence of mind and perfect command of the language, her heart meanwhile torn with anxiety for the loved one they might never see again.

Long and trying were the negotiations that followed, before the Yangchow house was repaired and the party permitted to return. Quite a function was arranged for their reception, and it was with thankfulness the leader of the Mission was able to write: "The results of this case will in all probability greatly facilitate work in the interior." But it was the family life and friendly spirit of the missionaries that gradually disarmed suspicion. "Actions speak louder than words," and neighbors had something to think over when the children were brought back after all that had happened, and when it appeared that Mrs. Taylor had not hesitated to return under conditions which made peace and quietness specially desirable.

In this again [she wrote to her beloved friend at Saint Hill] God has given me the desire of my heart. For I felt that if safety to my infant permitted it, I would rather it were born in this city, in this house, in this very room than in any other place—your own beautiful home not excepted, in which I have been so tenderly cared for, and the comforts and luxuries of which I know so well how to appreciate.

The arrival of a fourth son could not but make a favorable impression, as did the speedy recovery of all who had been injured in the riot. But far deeper was the compensation of finding that the inn-keeper who had first received them in the city, and two others who had dared much to befriend them during the riot, were now confessed believers in Christ and candidates for baptism.

"He that goeth forth and weepeth, bearing precious seed, shall doubtless come again with rejoicing, bringing his sheaves with him."

13

DAYS OF DARKNESS

Against me earth and hell combine;
But on my side is Power Divine;
Jesus is all, and He is mine.

—W. T. Matson

AT HOME IN ENGLAND, Mr. Berger was facing even a worse storm that winter than had
broken over the little mission in China. For the
Yangchow riot had stirred up criticism in Parlia-
ment and throughout the country to an extent that
seems hardly credible. Based upon misunderstandings, the public press was bitter in its attack upon
missionaries who had brought the country to the
verge of war with China, it was stated, demanding
the protection of British gunboats in their campaign
to induce the Chinese to change their religion "at
the mouth of the cannon and point of the bayonet."
Needless to say, Mr. Taylor and his colleagues had
given little if any ground for such criticism. Their
case had been taken up by the consular authorities
in a way that the missionaries neither expected nor
desired. Acting under instructions from the For-

eign Office, its representatives were quick to make
the most of the opportunity to press for treaty
rights, but before the not unreasonable demands of
the British Ambassador were complied with, a
change of Government in England complicated the
situation. Mrs. Taylor, writing to relieve her husband, put all the details fully before Mr. and Mrs.
Berger.

> As to the harsh judgings of the world [she con-
> cluded] or the more painful misunderstandings of
> Christian brethren, we generally feel that the best
> plan is to go on with our work and leave it to
> God to vindicate our cause. But it is right that
> you should know intimately how we have acted
> and why. I would suggest, however, that it would
> be undesirable to *print* the fact that Mr. Medhurst,
> the Consul General, and through him Sir Ruther-
> ford Alcock took the matter up without applica-
> tion from us. The new Ministry at home censures
> those out here for the policy which the late Minis-
> try enjoined upon them. It would be ungenerous
> and ungrateful were we to render their position
> still more difficult by throwing all the onus, so to
> speak, on them.

There was nothing for it but with prayer and
patience to weather the storm which continued long
after peaceful residence had been resumed at Yangchow. Four months later, indeed, Mr. Berger was
writing from Saint Hill.

> The Yangchow matter is before the House of
> Lords. . . . You can scarcely imagine what an effect
> it is producing in the country. Thank God I can

say, "None of these things move me." I believe He
has called us to this work, and it is not for us to
run away from it or allow difficulties to overcome
us. . . . Be of good courage, the battle is the Lord's.

It was doubly painful that, at such a crisis, the
disaffection of certain members of the Mission came
to a climax and the resignation had to be asked for
of some who from the very first had caused trouble.
Their representation of matters added to the misunderstandings at home, and in spite of Mr. Berger's
wise, strong leadership not a few friends were more
or less alienated from the work. This, together with
the strictures in the public press, affected the income in a serious way, so that the trials that pressed
upon the leaders of the Mission were neither few
nor small.

Pray for us [Mr. Taylor wrote soon after the
riot]. We need much grace. You cannot conceive
the daily calls there are for patience, for forbear-
ance, for tact in dealing with the many difficulties
and misunderstandings that arise among so many
persons of different nationality, language and
temperament. Pray the Lord ever to give me the
single eye, the clear judgment, the wisdom and
gentleness, the patient spirit, the unwavering purpose, the unshaken faith, the Christlike love needed
for the efficient discharge of my duties. And ask
Him to send us sufficient means and suitable helpers for the great work which we have as yet barely
commenced.

For in the midst of it all there was no halting in
the pioneer evangelism to which the Mission was

called. Even before Yangchow matters were settled,
Mr. Taylor had taken an important journey up the
Grand Canal to a city from which he hoped to reach
the northern provinces, and Mr. Meadows had left
his work in Ningpo to others that he might lead
an advance into the first inland province westward from Chinkiang—Anhwei with its twenty millions among whom there was not a single Protestant
missionary.

But instead of the increase of men and means for
which they were praying, there was a marked dim-
inution in the funds reaching them from home.
Unforeseen on their part, the situation was not un-
prepared for, however, as they found to their encouragement. For the One who had permitted the
troubles to come had also made provision in His
own wonderful way.

A penniless man in England—literally with no
more resources than the birds of the air or lilies of
the field—was already supporting through prayer
and faith a family of some two thousand orphan
children, later increased to double that number.
Without a cent of endowment, without an appeal
of any kind for help, without even letting their
wants be known to anyone but the Father in Heav-
en, on whose promise he relied, George Mueller
was proving the faithfulness of God in a way that
had long stimulated Hudson Taylor's faith and that
of many another. But so large was the heart of this
man of God in Bristol that he could not be content
without having some part in direct missionary work

in the darker places of the earth. He praved for funds with which he might forward the preaching of the Gospel in many lands, including China, and had the joy of being the Lord's channel of help in many a difficult situation. It seemed as if the Lord had his ear in quite a special way, and could use him in needed ministries that others overlooked or were not prepared for.

No sooner had the Yangchow riot taken place, for example, and long before the news could have reached England, it was laid on Mr. Mueller's heart to send financial help to the China Inland Mission. He was already contributing, but within a day or two of the riot he wrote to Mr. Berger asking for the names of other members of the Mission whom he might add to his list for ministry and prayer. Mr. Berger sent him six names from which to choose, and his choice was to take them all.

And then, a year later, when the shortness of funds in China was being most seriously felt, Mr. Mueller wrote again, enlarging his help. While that letter was on its way, Mr. Taylor, in sending out a December remittance, wrote to one of the workers:

> Over a thousand pounds *less* has been contributed during the first half of this (financial) year than last year. I do not keep a cook now. I find it cheaper to have cooked food brought in from an eating-house at a dollar a head per month. . . . Let us pray in faith for funds, that we may not have to diminish our work.

To diminish one's comforts seemed to him of small account, but "to diminish our work"—well, thank God, that was something he never had to do! Before the year closed, on this occasion, Mr. Mueller's letter was in his hands.

My dear Brother [it read], the work of the Lord in China is more and more laid on my heart, and hence I have been longing and praying to be able to assist it more and more with means, as well as with prayer. Of late I have especially had a desire to help all the dear brethren and sisters with you with pecuniary means. This I desired especially that they might see that I was interested in them personally. This my desire the Lord has now fulfilled.

The eleven checks enclosed were for all the members of the Mission to whom Mr. Mueller had not previously been ministering. Writing by the same mail, Mr. Berger said:

Mr. Mueller, after due consideration, has requested the names of *all* the brethren and sisters connected with the C.I.M., as he thinks it well to send help as he is able to each one, unless we know of anything to hinder. . . . Surely the Lord knew that our funds were sinking, and thus put it into the heart of His honoured servant to help.

But it was not the money only, it was the prayerful sympathy of such a man that made his gifts the wonderful encouragement they were.[1]

------

[1]Mr. Mueller's donations for the next few years amounted to nearly ten thousand dollars annually—just the sum by which the income of the Mission had fallen off after the Yangchow riot.

My chief object [he wrote in his letter to the missionaries] is to tell you that I love you in the Lord; that I feel deeply interested about the Lord's work in China, and that I pray daily for you.

I thought it might be a little encouragement to you in your difficulties, trials, hardships and disappointments to hear of one more who feels for you and who remembers you before the Lord. But were it otherwise, had you even no one to care for you—or did you at least seem to be in a position as if no one cared for you—you will always have the Lord to be with you. Remember Paul's case at Rome (2 Tim. 4:16-18).

On Him then reckon, to Him look, on Him depend: and be assured that if you walk with Him, look to Him and expect help from Him, He will never fail you. An older brother, who has known the Lord for forty-four years, who writes this, says for your encouragement that He has never failed him. In the greatest difficulties, in the heaviest trials, in the deepest poverty and necessities, He has never failed me; but because I was enabled by His grace to trust in Him, He has always appeared for my help. I delight in speaking well of His Name.

Sorely had such encouragement been needed by Mr. Taylor himself, for, strange as it may seem, the trouble that followed the Yangchow riot had been light compared with the trials within. Perhaps it was partly stress of outward circumstances that had hindered spiritual joy and rest; and yet, after the deeper experience that was drawing nearer, no amount of trial ever clouded his rejoicing in the Lord.

"It doesn't matter, really, how great the pressure is," he used to say; "it only matters *where the pressure lies*. See that it never comes *between* you and the Lord—then, the greater the pressure, the more it presses you to His breast."

But at that time he had not learned the secret that made his after life so radiant, and many were the hours of inward darkness and almost despair.

I have often asked you to remember me in prayer [he wrote to his mother], and when I have done so there has been much need of it. That need has never been greater than at present. Envied by some, despised by many, hated by others, often blamed for things I never heard of or had nothing to do with, an innovator on what have become established rules of missionary practice, an opponent of mighty systems of heathen error and superstition, working without precedent in many respects and with few experienced helpers, often sick in body as well as perplexed in mind and embarrassed by circumstances—had not the Lord been specially gracious to me, had not my mind been sustained by the conviction that the work is His and that He is with me in what it is no empty figure to call "the thick of the conflict," I must have fainted or broken down. But the battle *is* the Lord's, and He will conquer. We may fail—do fail continually—but He never fails. Still, I need your prayers more than ever.

My position becomes continually more and more responsible, and my need greater of special grace to fill it. But I have continually to mourn that I follow at such a distance and learn so slowly to imitate my precious Master.

I cannot tell you how I am buffeted sometimes by temptation. I never knew how bad a heart I have. Yet I do know that I love God and love His work, and desire to serve Him only and in all things. And I value above all else that precious Saviour in whom alone I can be accepted. Often I am tempted to think that one so full of sin cannot be a child of God at all. But I try to throw it back, and rejoice all the more in the preciousness of Jesus and in the riches of the grace that has made us "accepted in the beloved." Beloved He *is* of God; beloved He ought to be of us. But oh, how short I fall here again! May God help me to love Him more and serve Him better. Do pray for me. Pray that the Lord will keep me from sin, will sanctify me wholly, will use me more largely in His service.

"The Holy Spirit never creates hungerings and thirstings after righteousness, but in order that Christ may fill the longing soul."

"Faith in Jesus crucified is the way of peace to the sinner; so faith in Jesus risen is the way of daily salvation to the saint."

"You cannot be your own Saviour, either in whole or in part."

14

THE EXCHANGED LIFE

Yes, in me, in me He dwelleth—
I in Him and He in me!
And my empty soul He filleth
Now and through eternity.

—H. BONAR

SIX MONTHS AFTER the foregoing letter was written, a junk northward bound on the Grand Canal was carrying a passenger whose heart overflowed with a great, new-found joy. Mr. Judd in Yangchow was expecting the return of his friend and leader, but was hardly prepared for the transformation which had taken place in the one he knew so well. Scarcely waiting for greetings, Mr. Taylor plunged into his story. In characteristic fashion—his hands behind his back—he walked up and down the room exclaiming,

"Oh, Mr. Judd, God has made me a new man! God has made me a new man!"

Wonderful was the experience that had come in answer to prayer, yet so simple as almost to baffle

154

description. It was just as it was long ago, "Whereas I was blind, now I see!"

Amid a pile of letters awaiting Mr. Taylor in Chinkiang, had been one from John McCarthy, written in the old home in Hangchow. The glory of a great sunrise was upon him—the inward light whose dawning makes all things new. To tell Mr. Taylor about it was his longing, for he knew something of the exercise of soul through which his friend was passing. But where to begin, how to put it into words he knew not.

I do wish I could have a talk with you now [he wrote], about the way of holiness. At the time you were speaking to me about it, it was the subject of all others occupying my thoughts, not from anything I had read . . . so much as from a consciousness of failure—a constant falling short of that which I felt should be aimed at; an unrest; a perpetual striving to find some way by which one might continually enjoy that communion, that fellowship, at times so real but more often so visionary, so far off! . . .

Do you know, I now think that this striving, longing, hoping for better days to come is not the true way to holiness, happiness or usefulness. It is better, no doubt, far better than being satisfied with poor attainments, but not the best way after all. I have been struck with a passage from a book . . . entitled *Christ Is All*. It says,

"The Lord Jesus received is holiness begun; the Lord Jesus cherished is holiness advancing; the

Lord Jesus counted upon as never absent would be holiness complete. . . .

"He is most holy who has most of Christ within, and joys most fully in the finished work. It is defective faith which clogs the feet and causes many a fall."

This last sentence, I think I now fully endorse. To let my loving Saviour work in me His will, my sanctification, is what I would live for by His grace. Abiding, not striving nor struggling; looking off unto Him; trusting Him for present power; . . . resting in the love of an almighty Saviour, in the joy of a complete salvation, "from *all* sin"—this is not new, and yet 'tis *new to me*. I feel as though the dawning of a glorious day had risen upon me. I hail it with trembling, yet with trust. I seem to have got to the edge only, but of a boundless sea; to have sipped only, but of that which fully satisfies. Christ literally *all* seems to me, now, the power, the only power for service, the only ground for unchanging joy. . . .

How then to have our faith increased? Only by thinking of all that Jesus is and all He is for us: His life, His death, His work, He Himself as revealed to us in the Word, to be the subject of our constant thoughts. Not a striving to have faith . . . but a looking off to the Faithful One seems all we need; a resting in the Loved One entirely, for time and for eternity.

We do not know just how the miracle was wrought; but, "As I read, I saw it all," Mr. Taylor wrote. "I looked to Jesus, and when I saw—oh, how joy flowed!"

He was a joyous man now [Mr. Judd recorded], a bright happy Christian. He had been a toiling, burdened one before, with latterly not much rest of soul. It was resting in Jesus now, and letting Him do the work—which makes all the difference. Whenever he spoke in meetings after that, a new power seemed to flow from him, and in the practical things of life a new peace possessed him. Troubles did not worry him as before. He cast everything on God in a new way, and gave more time to prayer. Instead of working late at night, he began to go to bed earlier, rising at 5 A. M. to give time to Bible study and prayer (often two hours) before the work of the day began.

It was *the exchanged life* that had come to him— the life that is indeed "No longer I." Six months earlier he had written, "I have continually to mourn that I follow at such a distance and learn so slowly to imitate my precious Master." There was no thought of imitation now! It was in blessed reality "Christ liveth in me." And how great the difference!—instead of bondage, liberty; instead of failure, quiet victories within; instead of fear and weakness, a restful sense of sufficiency in Another. So great was the deliverance, that from that time onward Mr. Taylor could never do enough to help to make this precious secret plain to hungry hearts wherever he might be. And there are so many hungry hearts that need such help today that we venture to quote at length from one of his first letters on the subject. It was to his sister, Mrs. Broomhall, whose burdens with a family which grew to number ten children were very real and pressing.

So many thanks for your dear, long letter. . . . I do not think you have written me such a letter since our return to China. I know it is with you as with me—you cannot—not you will not. Mind and body will not bear more than a certain amount of strain, or do more than a certain amount of work.

As to work—mine was never so plentiful, so responsible or so difficult, but the weight and strain are all *gone*. The last month or more has been, perhaps, the happiest of my life, and I long to tell you a little of what the Lord has done for my soul. I do not know how far I may be able to make myself intelligible about it, for there is nothing new or strange or wonderful—and yet, all is new! . . .

Perhaps I may make myself more clear if I go back a little. Well, dearie, my mind has been greatly exercised for six or eight months past, feeling the need personally and for our Mission of more holiness, life, power in our souls. But personal need stood first and was the greatest. I felt the ingratitude, the danger, the sin of not living nearer to God. I prayed, agonized, fasted, strove, made resolutions, read the Word more diligently, sought more time for meditation—but all without avail. Every day, almost every hour, the consciousness of sin oppressed me.

I knew that if only I could abide in Christ all would be well, but I could not. I would begin the day with prayer, determined not to take my eye off Him for a moment, but pressure of duties, sometimes very trying, and constant interruptions apt to be so wearing, caused me to forget Him. Then one's nerves get so fretted in this climate that temptations to irritability, hard thoughts and sometimes unkind words are all the more difficult to control. Each day brought its register of sin and failure, of lack of power. To will was indeed "present with me," but how to perform I found not.

Then came the question, is there no rescue? Must it be thus to the end—constant conflict, and too often defeat? How could I preach with sincerity that, to those who receive Jesus, "to them gave he power to become the sons of God" (i.e., Godlike) when it was not so in my own experience? Instead of growing stronger, I seemed to be getting weaker and to have less power against sin; and no wonder, for faith and even hope were getting low. I hated myself, I hated my sin, yet gained no strength against it. I felt I *was* a child of God. His Spirit in my heart would cry, in spite of all, "Abba, Father." But to rise to my privileges as a child, I was utterly powerless.

I thought that holiness, practical holiness, was to be gradually attained by a diligent use of the means of grace. There was nothing I so much desired as holiness, nothing I so much needed; but far from in any measure attaining it, the more I strove after it, the more it eluded my grasp, until hope itself almost died out, and I began to think that— perhaps to make heaven the sweeter—God would not give it down here. I do not think that I was striving to attain it in my own strength. I knew I was powerless. I told the Lord so, and asked Him to give me help and strength. Sometimes I almost believed that He would keep and uphold me; but on looking back in the evening—alas! there was but sin and failure to confess and mourn before God.

I would not give you the impression that this was the only experience of those long, weary months. It was a too frequent state of soul, and that towards which I was tending, which almost ended in despair. And yet, never did Christ seem more precious; a Saviour who could and would save such a sinner! . . . And sometimes there were seasons not only of peace but of joy in the Lord; but they were transitory, and at best there was a sad lack of power. Oh, how good the Lord has been in bringing this conflict to an end!

All the time I felt assured that there was in Christ all I needed, but the practical question was —how to get it *out*. He was rich truly, but I was poor; He was strong, but I weak. I knew full well that there was in the root, the stem, abundant fatness, but how to get it into my puny little branch was the question. As gradually light dawned, I saw that faith was the only requisite—was the hand to lay hold on His fulness and make it mine. But I had not this faith.

I strove for faith, but it would not come; I tried to exercise it, but in vain. Seeing more and more the wondrous supply of grace laid up in Jesus, the fulness of our precious Saviour, my guilt and helplessness seemed to increase. Sins committed appeared but as trifles compared with the sin of unbelief which was their cause, which could not or would not take God at His word, but rather made Him a liar! Unbelief was I felt *the* damning sin of the world; yet I indulged in it. I prayed for faith, but it came not. What was I to do?

When my agony of soul was at its height, a sentence in a letter from dear McCarthy was used to remove the scales from my eyes, and the Spirit of God revealed to me the truth of our *oneness with Jesus* as I had never known it before. McCarthy, who had been much exercised by the same sense of failure but saw the light before I did, wrote (I quote from memory):

"But how to get faith strengthened? Not by striving after faith, but by resting on the Faithful One."

As I read, I saw it all! "If we believe not, he abideth faithful." I looked to Jesus and saw (and when I saw, oh, how joy flowed!) that He had said, "I will never leave thee."

"Ah, *there* is rest!" I thought. "I have striven in vain to rest in Him. I'll strive no more. For has not *He* promised to abide with *me*—never to leave me, never to fail me?" And, dearie, *He never will.*

Nor was this all He showed me, nor one half. As I thought of the Vine and the branches, what light the blessed Spirit poured direct into my soul! How great seemed my mistake in wishing to get the sap, the fulness *out* of Him! I saw not only that Jesus will never leave me, but that I am a member of His body, of His flesh and of His bones. The vine is not the root merely, but *all*—root, stem, branches, twigs, leaves, flowers, fruit. And Jesus is not that alone—He is soil and sunshine, air and showers, and ten thousand times more than we have ever dreamed, wished for or needed. Oh, the joy of seeing this truth! I do pray that the eyes of your understanding too may be enlightened, that you may know and enjoy the riches freely given us in Christ.

Oh, my dear Sister, it is a wonderful thing to be really one with a risen and exalted Saviour, to be a member of Christ! Think what it involves. Can Christ be rich and I poor? Can your right hand be rich and your left poor? or your head be well fed while your body starves? Again, think of its bearing on prayer. Could a bank clerk say to a customer, "It was only your hand, not you that wrote that check"; or "I cannot pay this sum to your hand, but only to yourself"? No more can your prayers or mine be discredited if offered in the name of Jesus (i.e., not for the sake of Jesus merely, but on the ground that we are His, His members) so long as we keep within the limits of Christ's credit—a tolerably wide limit! If we ask for anything unscriptural, or not in accordance with the will of God, Christ Himself could not do that. But "if we ask any thing according to his will . . . we know that we have the petitions that we desired of him."

The sweetest part, if one may speak of one part being sweeter than another, is the rest which full identification with Christ brings. I am no longer anxious about anything, as I realize this; for He, I know, is able to carry out His will, and His will is mine. It makes no matter where He places me, or how. That is rather for Him to consider than for me; for in the easiest position He must give me His grace, and in the most difficult His grace is sufficient. It little matters to my servant whether I send him to buy a few cash worth of things, or the most expensive articles. In either case he looks to me for the money and brings me his purchases. So, if God should place me in serious perplexity, must He not give me much guidance; in positions of great difficulty, much grace; in circumstances of great pressure and trial, much strength? No fear that His resources will prove unequal to the emergency! And His resources are mine, for He is mine, and is with me and dwells in me.

And since Christ has thus dwelt in my heart by faith, how happy I have been! I wish I could *tell* you about it, instead of writing. *I* am no better than before. In a sense, I do not wish to be, nor am I striving to be. But I am dead and buried with Christ—ay, and risen too! And now Christ lives in me, and "the life that I now live in the flesh, I live by the faith of the Son of God, who loved me and gave himself for me." . . .

And now I must close. I have not said half I would, nor *as* I would, had I more time. May God give you to lay hold on these blessed truths. Do not let us continue to say, in effect, "Who shall ascend into heaven? (that is, to bring Christ down from above)." In other words, do not let us consider Him as far off, when God has made us one with Him, members of His very body. Nor should we look upon this experience, these truths, as for the few. They are the birthright of every child of God, and no one can dispense with them without dishonouring our Lord. The only power for deliverance from sin or for true service is *Christ*.

And it was all so simple and practical!—as the busy mother found when she too entered into this rest of faith.

"But are you always conscious of abiding in Christ?" Mr. Taylor was asked many years later.

"While sleeping last night," he replied, "did I cease to abide in your home because I was unconscious of the fact? We should never be conscious of *not* abiding in Christ."

> I change, He changes not;
>   The Christ can never die:
> His truth, not mine, the resting place;
>   His love, not mine, the tie.

15

NO MORE THIRST

What then? I am not careful to inquire:
  I know there will be tears and fears and sorrow—
And then a loving Saviour drawing nigher,
  And saying, "I will answer for the morrow."

—Selected

IT WAS AN EXPERIENCE that stood the test, as months and years went by. Never again did the unsatisfied days come back; never again was the needy soul separated from the fullness of Christ. Trials came, deeper and more searching then ever before, but in them all joy flowed unhindered from the presence of the Lord Himself. For Hudson Taylor had found the secret of soul-rest. In this experience there had come to him not only a fuller apprehension of the Lord Jesus Himself and all He is for us, but a fuller surrender—yes, indeed, a self-abandonment to Him.

I am no longer anxious about anything [he had written, as we have seen] . . . for He, I know, is able to carry out His will, and His will is mine. It makes no matter where He places me, or how.

That is rather for Him to consider than for me; for in the easiest position He must give me His grace, and in the most difficult His grace is sufficient. It little matters to my servant whether I send him to buy a few cash worth of things or the most expensive articles. In either case he looks to me for the money and brings me his purchases. So, if God should place me in great perplexity, must He not give me much guidance; in positions of great difficulty, much grace; in circumstances of great pressure and trial, much strength? No fear that His resources will be unequal to the emergency! And His resources are mine—for He is mine, and is with me and dwells in me.

Surrender to Christ he had long known, but this was more; this was a new yieldedness, a glad, unreserved handing over of self and everything to Him. It was no longer a question of giving up this or that if the Lord required it; it was a loyal and loving acceptance, a joyful meeting of His will in things little and great, as the very best that could be for His own. This made the trials of the following summer an opportunity for God's grace to triumph, turning "the valley of weeping" into "a place of springs" from which streams of blessing are flowing still.

Even before the danger and excitement that culminated in the massacre of Tientsin, Mr. and Mrs. Taylor had been called to pass through deep personal sorrow. The time had come when the inevitable parting from their children could no longer be delayed. There were no schools in China at which their education could be carried on, and no health resorts such as there are now for refuge from the heat of summer. The climate and privations of their life had told upon the children's health. One little grave already hallowed the soil of China to the parents' hearts, and they were thankful to accept the offer of their secretary and devoted friend, Miss Emily Blatchley, to take the three boys and only little girl to England and to care for them there.

This meant a long, long parting, and East and West were so much farther apart then than they are now! But even before the little travelers could be escorted to the coast, a longer parting still had to be faced. Only five years old, the youngest of the boys, a specially clinging little fellow, was the one whose health had suffered most. With concern his parents saw that the strain of the coming separation was increasing his chronic trouble. All night they watched beside him on the boat that was taking them down the canal from Yangchow, but at dawn the following morning he fell into a deep sleep, and from the turbid waters of the Yangtze passed without pain or fear to the better land.

Before a driving storm the parents crossed the river—there about two miles wide—to lay their treasure in the cemetery at Chinkiang, and then went on with the others to Shanghai. A little later, after taking them all on board the French mail which was to sail at daylight, Mr. Taylor wrote to Mr. Berger:

I have seen them, awake, for the last time in China. [He was returning to fetch Mrs. Taylor who was still on the steamer.] About two of our little ones we have no anxiety. They rest in Jesus' bosom. And now, dear brother, though the tears will not be stayed, I do thank God for permitting one so unworthy to take any part in this great work, and do not regret having engaged in it. It is His work, not mine or yours; and yet it is ours —not because we are engaged in it, but because we are His, and one with Him whose work it is.

This was the reality that sustained them. Never had there been a more troubled summer in China than the one on which they were entering (1870). Yet in the midst of it all, with a longing for their children that was indescribable, they had never had more rest and joy in God.

I could not but admire and wonder at the grace that so sustained and comforted the fondest of mothers [Mr. Taylor wrote as he recalled it afterwards]. The secret was that Jesus was *satisfying* the deep thirst of heart and soul.

Mrs. Taylor was at her best that summer, borne up it would seem on the very tempest of troubles that raged about them. Sickness was rife in the Mission, and before they could reach Chinkiang, after parting from the children, news reached them of Mrs. Judd's being there and at the point of death. Mr. Taylor could not leave the boat on account of another patient, but consented to Mrs. Taylor's pressing on alone to give what help she could.

After days and nights of nursing, Mr. Judd was

almost at the end of his strength, when he heard sounds in the courtyard below of an unexpected arrival. Who could it be at that time of night and where had they come from? No steamer had passed upriver, and native boats would not be traveling after dark. Besides, it was a wheelbarrow that had been trundled in. A long day's journey on that springless barrow, a woman had come alone, and soon he saw the face that of all others he could have desired to see.

Suffering though Mrs. Taylor was at the time [he recalled] and worn with hard travelling, she insisted on my going to bed and that she would undertake the nursing. Nothing would induce her to rest.

"No," she said, "you have quite enough to bear without sitting up at night any more. Go to bed, for I shall stay with your wife whether you do or not."

Never can I forget the firmness and love with which it was said—her face meanwhile shining with the tenderness of Him in whom it was her joy and strength to abide.

Nothing but prayer brought the patient through, just as nothing but prayer saved the situation in many an hour of extremity that summer.

We had previously known something of trial in one station or another [Mr. Taylor wrote to the friends of the Mission], but now in all simultaneously, or nearly so, a widespread excitement shook the very foundations of native society. It is impossible to describe the alarm and consternation of the Chinese when they first believed that native magicians were bewitching them, or their indignation and anger when told that these insidious foes were the agents of foreigners. It is well known how in Tientsin they rose and barbarously murdered the Sisters of Charity, the priests and even the French Consul. What then restrained them in the interior, where our brothers were alone, far from any protecting human power? Nothing but *the mighty hand of God,* in answer to united, constant prayer in the all-prevailing name of Jesus. And this same power kept *us* satisfied with Jesus—with His presence, His love, His providence.

It is easy to read of such experiences, but only those who have lived through similar times of danger can have any idea of the strain involved. The heat that summer was unusually severe and prolonged, which added to the unrest of the native population. Women and children had to be brought down to the coast, and for a time it seemed as though the Chinese authorities might require them to leave the country altogether. This involved much correspondence with officials, Chinese and foreign, and frequent letters to the workers most in peril. The accommodation of the Mission house at Chinkiang was taxed to its utmost, and so great was the excitement that no additional premises could be obtained.

Old times seem to be coming round again [Mr. Taylor wrote in June, referring to the Yangchow riot], but with this difference that our anxieties are not as before confined to one place.

By this time it looked as though all the river stations might have to be given up. Mr. and Mrs. Taylor were making their home at Chinkiang as more central than Yangchow, he sleeping on the floor in sitting-room or passage that she might share their room with other ladies.

One difficulty follows another very fast [he continued after the Tientsin massacre], but God reigns, not chance. At Nanking the excitement has been frightful. . . . Here the rumours are, I hope, passing away, but at Yangchow they are very bad. . . . Pray much for us. My heart is calm, but my head is sorely tried by the constant succession of one difficulty after another.

Yet the troubles of the time were not allowed to hinder the spiritual side of the work, in which Mr. and Mrs. Taylor took their full share. In the hottest days of June the latter wrote to Miss Blatchley:

We have been holding classes on Sunday and two or three evenings in the week, to interest the Chinese Christians who can read, in searching the Scriptures, and those who cannot read in learning to do so, and to set an example to the younger members of the Mission who know pretty well that we have no lack of work. It may be a practical proof to them of the importance we attach to securing that the Christians and others about us learn to read and understand for themselves the Word of God.

The joy that had come to Mr. Taylor in his spiritual experience seems to have been deepened rather than hindered by the exigencies of the time.

His letter-book reveals not so much the pressure of difficulties and problems as the full tide of blessing that carried him through all. To Miss Desgraz he wrote, for example, in the middle of June, after carefully answering her letter about Yanchow affairs:

And now I have the very passage for you, and God has so blessed it to my own soul! John 7:37-39 —"If any man thirst, let him come unto ME and drink." Who does not thirst? Who has not mind-thirsts, heart-thirsts, soul-thirsts or body-thirsts? Well, no matter which, or whether I have them all— "Come unto me and" remain thirsty? Ah no! "Come unto me and *drink*."

What, can Jesus meet my need? Yes, and more than meet it. No matter how intricate my path, how difficult my service; no matter how sad my bereavement, how far away my loved ones; no matter how helpless I am, how deep are my soul-yearnings—Jesus can meet all, all, and more than *meet*. He not only promises me rest—ah, how welcome that would be, were it all, and what an all that one word embraces! He not only promises me drink to alleviate my thirst. No, better than that! "He who trusts Me in this matter (who believeth on Me, takes Me at My word) out of him shall *flow* . . ."

Can it be? Can the dry and thirsty one not only be refreshed—the parched soil moistened, the arid places cooled—but the land be so saturated that springs well up and streams flow down from it? Even so! And not mere mountain-torrents, full while the rain lasts, then dry again . . . but, "from

within him shall flow rivers"—rivers like the mighty
Yangtze, ever deep, ever full. In times of drought
brooks may fail, often do, canals may be pumped
dry, often are, but the Yangtze never. Always a
mighty stream, always flowing deep and irresist-
ible!

"Come unto me and drink," [he wrote in another June letter]. Not, come and take a hasty
draught; not, come and slightly alleviate, or for a
short time remove one's thirst. No! "drink," or
"be drinking" constantly, habitually. The cause of
thirst may be irremediable. One coming, one drinking may refresh and comfort: but we are to be ever
coming, ever drinking. No fear of emptying the
fountain or exhausting the river!

How sorely the comfort of Christ would be
needed by his own heart that very summer, he little
realized when writing; but the One he was trusting
in a new and deeper way did not fail him.

* * * * *

Six weeks later, joy and sorrow were strangely
mingled in the missionary home at Chinkiang. A
little son given to Mr. and Mrs. Taylor had filled
their hearts with gladness. But an attack of cholera
greatly prostrated the mother, and lack of natural
nourishment told upon the infant. When a Chinese
nurse could be found, it was too late to save the
little life, and after only one week on earth he went
to the home above, in which his mother was so
soon to join him.

Though excessively prostrated in body [Mr. Taylor wrote], the deep peace of soul, the realization

of the Lord's own presence and joy in His holy
will with which she was filled, and which I was
permitted to share, I can find no words to describe.

She herself chose the hymns to be sung at the
funeral, one of which, "O holy Saviour, Friend unseen," seemed specially to dwell in her mind.

Though faith and hope are often tried,
They ask not, need not aught beside;
So safe, so calm, so satisfied,
    The souls that cling to Thee.

They fear not Satan or the grave,
They know Thee near and strong to save,
Nor fear to cross e'en Jordan's wave
    While still they cling to Thee.

Weak as she was, it had not occurred to them that
her days were numbered. The very love that bound
their hearts so closely precluded the thought of
separation. And she was only thirty-three. There
was no pain up to the last, only increasing weariness. Two days before the end, a letter from Mrs.
Berger came to hand, telling of the safe arrival at
Saint Hill of Miss Blatchley and the older children.[1]
Every detail of the welcome and arrangements for
their well-being filled the mother's heart with joy.
She could not be thankful enough, and seemed to
have no desire but to praise God for His goodness.
Many a time had Mrs. Berger's letters reached their
destination at the needed moment, many a time had
her loving heart anticipated the circumstances in

---

[1]One little one only remained with Mr. and Mrs. Taylor,
their fourth son, born soon after the Yangchow riot.

which they would be received, but never more so than with this letter.

"And now, farewell, precious friend," she wrote. "The Lord throw around you His everlasting arms."

It was in those arms she was resting.

I never witnessed such a scene [wrote one who was present]. As dear Mrs. Taylor was breathing her last, Mr. Taylor knelt and committed her to the Lord, thanking Him for having given her and for twelve and a half years of perfect happiness together, thanking Him too for taking her to His own presence, and solemnly dedicating himself anew to His service.

The summer sun rose higher over the city, hills and river. The busy hum of life came up around them from many a court and street. But in an upper room of one Chinese dwelling, from which the blue of heaven could be seen, there was the hush of a wonderful peace.

* * * * *

"Shall never thirst"—would it, could it prove true now? "To know that 'shall' means *shall,* that 'never' means *never,* and that 'thirst' means *any unsatisfied need,*" Mr. Taylor often said in later years, "may be one of the greatest revelations God ever made to our souls." It was in these days of utter desolation that the promise was made so real to his breaking heart.

To his mother he wrote in August:

From my inmost soul I delight in the knowledge that God does or permits *all* things, and causes all things to work together for good to those who love Him.

He and He only knew what my dear wife was to me. He knew how the light of my eyes and the joy of my heart were in her. On the last day of her life—we had *no* idea that it would be the last —our hearts were mutually delighted by the never-old story of each other's love . . . and almost her last act was, with one arm round my neck, to place her hand on my head and, as I believe, for her lips had lost their cunning, to implore a blessing on me. But He saw that it was good to take her— good indeed for her, and in His love He took her painlessly—and not less good for me who now must toil and suffer alone, yet not alone, for God is nearer to me than ever.

And to Mr. Berger:

When I think of my loss, my heart, nigh to breaking, rises in thankfulness to Him who has spared her such sorrow and made her so unspeak-ably happy. My tears are more tears of joy than grief. But most of all I joy in God through our Lord Jesus Christ—in His works, His ways, His providence, Himself. He is giving me to "prove" (to know by trial) "what is that good, and ac-ceptable, and perfect, will of God." I do rejoice in that will; it is acceptable to me; it is perfect; it is love in action. And soon, in that sweet will, we shall be reunited to part no more. "Father, I will that they also, whom thou hast given me, be with me where I am."

Yet there was a measure of reaction, especially when illness came with long, wakeful nights.

How lonesome [Mr. Taylor recalled] were the weary hours when confined to my room! How I

missed my dear wife and the voices of the children
far away in England!   Then it was I understood
why the Lord had made that passage so real to me,
"Whosoever drinketh of the water that I shall give
him *shall never thirst.*"   Twenty times a day, perhaps, as I felt the heart-thirst coming back, I cried
to Him,

"Lord, you promised!   You promised me that I
should never thirst."

And whether I called by day or night, how
quickly He came and satisfied my sorrowing heart!
So much so that I often wondered whether it were
possible that my loved one who had been taken
could be enjoying more of His presence than I was
in my lonely chamber.   He did literally fulfil the
prayer:

"Lord Jesus, make Thyself to me
A living, bright reality;
   More present to faith's vision keen
   Than any outward object seen;
More dear, more intimately nigh
Than e'en the sweetest earthly tie."

Among many letters of this period few are more
precious or revealing than those he managed to write
to the children, over whom his heart yearned with
a great love.

You do not know how often Father thinks of his
darlings, and how often he looks at your photo-
graphs till the tears fill his eyes.   Sometimes he almost fears lest he should feel discontented when he
thinks how far away you are from him.   But then
the dear Lord Jesus who never leaves him says,
"Don't be afraid: I will keep your heart satis-

fied." . . . And I thank Him, and am so glad that
He will live in my heart and keep it right for me.

I wish you, my precious children, knew what it is
to give your hearts to Jesus to keep every day. I
used to try to keep my own heart right, but it
would always be going wrong. So at last I had
to give up trying myself, and to accept the Lord's
offer to keep it for me. Don't you think that is
the best way? Perhaps sometimes you think, "I
will try not to be selfish or unkind or disobedient."
And yet, though you really try, you do not succeed.
But Jesus says: "You should trust that to Me. I
would keep that little heart, if you would trust Me
with it." And He would, too.

Once I used to try to think very much and very
often about Jesus, but I often forgot Him. Now I
trust Jesus to keep my heart remembering Him,
and He does so. This is the best way. Ask dear
Miss Blatchley to tell you more about this way, and
pray God to make it plain to you, and to help *you*
so to trust Jesus.

And to Miss Blatchley he wrote on the same subject, from the comfortless quarters of a coasting
steamer:

I have written again to the dear children. I do
long for them to learn early . . . the precious truths
which have come so late to me concerning oneness
with and the indwelling of Christ. These do not
seem to me more difficult of apprehension than the
truths about redemption. Both need the teaching
of the Spirit, nothing more. May God help you
to live Christ before these little ones, and to minister Him to them. How wonderfully He has led

and taught us! How little I believed the rest and
peace of heart I now enjoy were *possible* down
here! It is heaven begun below, is it not? . . .
Compared with this union with Christ, heaven or
earth are unimportant accidents.

Oh, it is joy to feel Jesus living in you [he wrote
to his sister, Mrs. Walker, on the same journey];
to find your heart all taken up by Him; to be reminded of His love by *His* seeking communion with
you at all times, not by your painful attempts to
abide in Him. He is our life, our strength, our salvation. He is our "wisdom, and righteousness, and
sanctification, and redemption." He is our power
for service and fruit-bearing, and His bosom is our
resting place now and forever.

There was, meanwhile no lessening of outward
difficulties. Politically the aspect of affairs was more
threatening than Mr. Taylor had ever known it in
China. The claims arising from the Tientsin massacre, in which twenty-one foreigners had lost their
lives, including the French Consul, were still un-
settled, and the Chinese authorities, knowing that
Europe was involved in war, took no steps to allay
the antiforeign agitation.[2] So closely, in some ways,

---

[2]"Never in my lifetime has any year witnessed such events,"
Mr. Berger wrote, "whether in relation to our Mission or the
world at large. Rome is now, I suppose, the capital of free
Italy. France lies humiliated in the last degree. The Pope's
temporal power is no more. China seems to be rising to
expel foreigners, the heralds of the Cross among them, and
we personally have suffered the loss of the most devoted
labourer for China's millions that could be found, as well as
of a most beloved friend. 'Be still, and know that I am
God' is a word appropriate at such a juncture. May we all
have grace to give heed to it."

did the situation resemble the present (1932)
though in miniature, that we venture to quote one
further letter showing the spirit in which the perils
of 1870 were met. For principles remain the same,
and as a Mission we stand today just where they
stood when Mr. Taylor sent out his call for the day
of fasting and prayer with which the year closed.

The present year has been in many ways remarkable. Perhaps every one of our number has
been more or less face to face with danger, perplexity and distress. But out of it all the Lord has
delivered us. And some who have drunk more
deeply than ever before of the cup of the Man of
Sorrows can testify that it has been a most blessed
year to our souls and can give God thanks for it.
Personally, it has been the most sorrowful and the
most blessed year of my life, and I doubt not that
others have had in some measure the same experience. We have put to the proof the faithfulness of
God—His power to support in trouble and to give
patience under affliction, as well as to deliver
from danger. And should greater dangers await us,
should deeper sorrows come . . . it is to be hoped
that they will be met in a strengthened confidence
in our God.

We have great cause for thankfulness in one re-
spect: we have been so situated as to show the
Chinese Christians that our position, as well as
theirs, has been and may again be one of danger.
They have been helped, doubtless, to look from
"foreign power" to God Himself for protection by
the fact that (1) the former has been felt to be

uncertain and unreliable . . . and (2) that we have
been kept in calmness and joy in our various positions of duty. If in any measure we have failed to
improve for their good this opportunity, or have
failed to rest, for ourselves, in God's power to sustain us in or protect us from danger, as He sees
best, let us humbly confess this, and all conscious
failure, to our faithful covenant-keeping God. . . .

I trust we are all fully satisfied that we are God's
servants, sent by Him to the various posts we occupy, and that we are doing His work in them. He
set before us the open doors we have entered, and
in past times of excitement He has preserved us.
We did not come to China because missionary work
here was either safe or easy, but because He had
called us. We did not enter upon our present
positions under a guarantee of human protection,
but relying on the promise of His presence. The
accidents of ease or difficulty, of apparent safety or
danger, of man's approval or disapproval, in no
wise affect our duty. Should circumstances arise
involving us in what may seem special danger, we
shall have grace, I trust, to manifest the depth and
reality of our confidence in Him, and by faithfulness to our charge to prove that we are followers
of the Good Shepherd who did not flee from death
itself. . . . But if we would manifest such a spirit
then, we must seek the needed grace *now.* It is
too late to look for arms and begin to drill when
in presence of the foe.

As to temporal supplies, Mr. Taylor continued:

I need not remind you of the liberal help which
the Lord has sent us direct, in our time of need,

from certain donors, nor of the blessed fact that
He abideth faithful and cannot deny Himself. If
we are really trusting in Him and seeking from
Him, we cannot be put to shame. If not, perhaps
the sooner we find out the unsoundness of any
other foundation, the better. The Mission funds,
or the donors, are a poor substitute for the living
God.

"Days of sorrow and nights of heaviness" did come
through a physical breakdown, early in 1871. Mr.
Taylor found that a badly deranged liver made him
sleepless and led to painful depression of spirit.
This was increased by chest trouble which caused
not only pain but serious difficulty in breathing.
And time did not lessen the sense of his loss. It
was under these circumstances that he discovered
fresh power and beauty in the promise already so
vital in his experience. "Whosoever *drinketh* of the
water that I shall give him"—the suggestion of a
continuous habit, indicated by the present tense of
the Greek verb, flooded the passage with new meaning and met his long-continued need.

Do not let us change the Saviour's words [he
often said in later years]. It is not "Whosoever
has drunk," but "Whosoever *drinketh*." It is not
of one isolated draught He speaks, or even many,
but of the continuous habit of the soul. In John
6:35, also, the full meaning is, "He who is habitually coming to me shall by no means hunger, and
he who is believing on me shall by no means thirst."
The habit of coming in faith to Him is incom-
patible with unmet hunger and thirst. . . .

It seems to me that where many of us err is in leaving our drinking in the past, while our thirst continues present.   What we need is *to be drinking* —yes, thankful for each occasion which drives us to drink ever more deeply of the living water.

16

OVERFLOW

In Thy strong hand I lay me down,
　So shall the work be done;
For who can work so wondrously
　As the Almighty One?

　　　　　　　　　　　　　—SELECTED

THIRTY YEARS of active life as Director of the
China Inland Mission remained to Mr. Taylor,
and more than thirty years have passed since he laid
down those responsibilities. Sixty years, the average
span of two generations, have given time to test
the tree by its fruit—to prove, in other words, what
has been the outcome of the faith and joy in God
in which his life was rooted. If the experiences
we have traced were emotional and unreal, if the
spiritual is not also the practical, if God is not sufficient for the needs of His own work, apart from
financial guarantees or human protection, then the
acid test of time will surely have dissolved the illu-
sions. But if Hudson Taylor, with all his limitations, had really found the secret of power and

blessing in living union with the Lord Jesus Christ, then the results remain—and will, to all eternity.

All things are possible to God,
    To Christ the power of God in man,
To me when I am all renewed,
    In Christ am fully formed again,
And from the reign of sin set free,—
All things are possible to me.

* * * * *

In the testing days of 1870, Hudson Taylor was still a young man in his thirties, and the Mission numbered only thirty-three members. Stations had been opened in three provinces and converts gathered into ten or twelve little churches. It was still a day of small things; yet the burden was considerable when it all came upon one man, and he already wearied with five such years in China.

For by the end of 1871, it became clear that Mr. and Mrs. Berger, who had so generously cared for the home side of the Mission, could no longer continue their strenuous labors. Failing health obliged them to winter abroad. Saint Hill was to be sold, and all the correspondence, account keeping and editorial work, the testing of candidates and practical management of business details must pass into other hands. The links of loving sympathy remained the same. But it was with a sense of almost desolation that Mr. Taylor took over the responsibility, which necessitated his remaining for a time in England.

It was a far cry from Saint Hill to Pyrland Road,

a little suburban street in the north of London, and the change from Mr. Berger's library to the small back room which had to do duty as study and office in one was no less complete. But how dear and sacred to many a heart is every remembrance of "Number Six" and the adjacent houses acquired as need arose! For more than twenty years the home work of the Mission was carried on from that center, a few steps only from its present headquarters. The weekly prayer meeting was held in the downstairs rooms, two of which could be thrown together, and many a devoted band of men and women, including "The Seventy" and "The Hundred," went forth from those doors. But we are running far ahead of the small beginnings of 1872, when Mr. Taylor himself was the sole executive of the Mission, as well as the Director of its work in China.

My path is far from easy [he wrote early that year]. I never was more happy in Jesus, and I am very sure He will not fail us; but never from the foundation of the Mission have we been more cast upon God. It is well, doubtless, that it should be so. Difficulties afford a platform upon which He can show Himself. Without them we could never know how tender, faithful and almighty our God is. . . . The change about Mr. and Mrs. Berger has tried me not a little. I love them so dearly! And it seems another link severed with the past in which my precious departed one, who is seldom absent from my thoughts, had a part. But His word is, "Behold, I make all things new."

Longing to press forward with the great task be-

fore the Mission, it must have been difficult indeed
for Mr. Taylor to curb himself to the routine of
office work as days and weeks went by. He was not
in haste to rush into new arrangements, having no
indication as to what the Lord had in view. But
when prayer for the right helpers seemed to bring
no answer, and the work to be done kept him from
what he was tempted to regard as more important
matters, it would have been easy to be impatient or
discouraged. With one in similar trial he sought
to share some of the lessons he was learning.

It is no small comfort to me to know that God
has called me to my work, putting me where I am
and as I am. I have not sought the position and
I dare not leave it. He knows why He places me
here—whether to do, or learn, or suffer. "He that
believeth shall not make haste." That is no easy
lesson for you or me; but I honestly think that ten
years would be well spent, and we should have our
full value for them, if we thoroughly learned it in
them. . . . Moses seems to have been taken aside
for forty years to learn it. . . . Meanwhile, let us
beware alike of the haste of the impatient, impetu-
ous flesh, and of its disappointment and weariness.

But this restricted life, because of its real fellowship with the Lord Jesus Christ, was bearing fruit,
and it is interesting to note the reaction of young
people especially to its influence. In the busy world
of London, a bright lad had given his heart to the
Lord and desired to learn about opportunities for
life-work in China. Making his way to Pyrland

Road, he found himself in the plainly furnished
room where people were gathering for the prayer
meeting.

A large text [he recalled] faced the door by
which we entered, "My God shall supply all your
need," and as I was not accustomed to seeing texts
hung on walls in that way, decidedly impressed
me. Between a dozen and twenty people were
present. . . .

Mr. Taylor opened the meeting by giving out
a hymn, and seating himself at the harmonium led
the singing. His appearance did not impress me.
He was slightly built, and spoke in a quiet voice.
Like most young men, I suppose I associated
power with noise, and looked for physical presence in a leader. But when he said, "Let us pray,"
and proceeded to lead the meeting in prayer, my
ideas underwent a change. I had never heard anyone pray like that. There was a simplicity, a tenderness, a boldness, a power that hushed and sub-
dued me, and made it clear that God had admit-
ted him to the inner circle of His friendship. Such
praying was evidently the outcome of long tarry-
ing in the secret place, and was as dew from the
Lord.

I have heard many men pray in public since
then, but the prayers of Mr. Taylor and the prayers
of Mr. Spurgeon stand all by themselves. Who that
heard could ever forget them? It was the experience of a lifetime to hear Mr. Spurgeon pray, taking as it were the great congregation of six thousand people by the hand and leading them into
the holy place. And to hear Mr. Taylor plead for

China was to know something of what is meant by
"the effectual fervent prayer of a righteous man."
That meeting lasted from four to six o'clock, but
seemed one of the shortest prayer meetings I had
ever attended.

From the west of England, a girl of education and
refinement had come up to London to attend the
Mildmay Conference, and was staying as a guest at
Pyrland Road. She heard Mr. Taylor give the opening address, when two to three thousand people
crowded the great hall, and saw how he influenced
leaders of Christian thought. But it was in the
everyday life of the Mission house hard by that he
impressed her most—bearing its burdens and meeting its tests of faith with daily joy in the Lord.

I remember Mr. Taylor's exhortation [Miss Soltau wrote long after] to keep silent to all around
and let our wants be known to God only. One
day, when we had had a small breakfast and there
was scarcely anything for dinner, I was thrilled
to hear him singing the children's hymn:

> "Jesus loves me, this I know,
> For the Bible tells me so."

Then he called us together to praise the Lord for
His changeless love, to tell our needs and claim
the promises. And before the day was over we
were rejoicing in His gracious answers.

Far from being discouraged by the shortness of
funds after Mr. Berger's retirement, Mr. Taylor was
looking forward more definitely than ever toward
advance. Standing before the big map of China one

day at Pyrland Road, he turned to a few friends who were with him and said:

"Have you faith to join me in laying hold upon God for eighteen men to go two and two to the nine unevangelized provinces?"

Miss Soltau was of the group and still recalls how they joined hands before the map, earnestly covenanting to pray daily for the eighteen evangelists needed until they should be given. There was no doubt about the faith. But how little any of them dreamed of the wider expansion that was coming; of the important part Miss Soltau herself was to take in the development of the Mission, or of the unique service to be rendered by F. W. Baller, the bright lad mentioned above—both drawn to the work at this time through the unconscious overflow of Mr. Taylor's life.

So the waiting time was fruitful, and when Mr. Taylor was able to return to China he left behind him a Council of long-tried friends in London, in addition to Miss Blatchley in charge of the home and children at Pyrland Road. It was not a large balance that he transferred to the honorary secretaries. Twenty-one pounds was all the money they had in hand. But there was no debt, and it was with confidence Mr. Taylor wrote to the friends of the Mission:

Now that the work has grown, more helpers are needed at home, as abroad, but the principles of action remain the same. We shall seek pecuniary aid from God by prayer, as heretofore. He will put it into the hearts of those He sees fit to use to act as His channels. When there is money in hand it will be remitted to China; when there is none, none will be sent; and we shall not draw upon home, so that there can be no going into debt. Should our faith be tried as it has been before, the Lord will prove Himself faithful as He has ever done. Nay, should our faith fail, His faithfulness will not—for it is written, "If we believe not, yet he abideth faithful."

Never was this confidence more needed than when, after an absence of fifteen months, the leader of the Mission found himself again in China. Through sickness and other hindrances, the work was discouraging in several of the older centers. Little churches were not what they had been; stations were undermanned, some even closed, and Mr. Taylor scarcely knew where to begin to give the help and encouragement needed. Instead of planning for advance to unreached provinces, it was all he could do to build up the existing work. Well was it, for his own comfort, that he had with him the devoted companion God had brought into his life. Miss Faulding, the much-loved leader of the women's work in Hangchow, had become his second wife, commencing the selfless ministry at his side which for thirty-three years endeared her to the entire fellowship of the Mission. But they were often parted. In wintry weather with snow deep on the ground, Mr. Taylor was thankful to spare her the journeys he himself had to take, often at no little cost.

I have invited the church members and inquirers to dine with me tomorrow [he wrote from one closed station]. I want them all to meet together. May the Lord give us His blessing. Though things are sadly discouraging, they are not hopeless; they will soon look up, by God's blessing, if they are looked after.

Very characteristic of the practical nature of Mr. Taylor's faith was that little word, "things will soon look up, by God's blessing, if they are looked after." Taking himself the hardest places, and depending on the quickening power of the Spirit, he went on prayerfully and patiently, straightening out difficulties and infusing new earnestness into converts and missionaries alike. Joined by Mrs. Taylor in the Yangtze valley, he spent three months at Nanking, giving much time to direct evangelism.

Every night we gather large numbers by means of pictures and lantern slides [he wrote from that city] and preach to them Jesus. . . . We had fully five hundred in the chapel last night. Some did not stay long; others were there nearly three hours. May the Lord bless our stay here to souls. . . . Every afternoon women come to see and hear.

Something of the inward sustaining may be gathered from a question in a letter to Miss Blatchley:

If you are ever drinking at the Fountain [he wrote] with what will your life be running over?— Jesus, Jesus, Jesus!

It was a full cup he carried, in this sense, and the overflow was just what was needed. So the visits accomplished their object, and were continued

until Mr. Taylor had been, once at any rate, at
every station, and almost every outstation in the
Mission. Not content with this, he sought out the
Chinese leaders in each place; and the evangelists,
colporteurs, teachers and Bible-women, almost without exception, were personally helped. When they
could be together, Mrs. Taylor's assistance was invaluable, and they would work at times far into the
night attending to correspondence. On medical
journeys she was often his companion; or she might
remain at one station where there was sickness,
while he went on to another. How glad they were
of his medical knowledge in those days, for there
was no other doctor in the Mission or anywhere
away from the treaty ports. Needless to say, it
added not a little to Mr. Taylor's burdens—as when
he reached a distant station to find ninety-eight letters awaiting him, and took time the very next day
to write a page of medical instructions about "A-
liang's baby," A-liang being a valued helper at
Chinkiang. But whether it meant longer letters or
extra journeys, he was thankful for any and every
way in which he could help. To be "the servant
of all" was the privilege he desired most.

The Lord is prospering us [he was able to write
after about nine months] and the work is steadily
growing, especially in that most important department, *native help*. The helpers themselves need
much help, much care and instruction; but they
are becoming more efficient as well as more numer-
ous, and the hope for China lies doubtless in *them*.

I look on foreign missionaries as the scaffolding round a rising building; the sooner it can be dispensed with the better—or the sooner, rather, that it can be transferred to serve the same temporary purpose elsewhere.

What prayer and vision went hand in hand with these unremitting labors! It would have been easy to lose the sense of *urgency* about the great need beyond, in the stress of needs at hand, especially when funds for the existing work were none too plentiful. But with Mr. Taylor, just the reverse was the case. Traveling from place to place, long journeys between the stations, through populous country teeming with friendly, accessible people, his heart went out more and more to the unreached, both near and far.

Last week I was at Taiping [he wrote to the Council in London]. My heart was greatly moved by the crowds that literally filled the streets for two or three miles, so that we could hardly walk, for it was market day. We did but little preaching, for we were looking for a place for permanent work, but I was constrained to retire to the city wall and cry to God to have mercy on the people, to open their hearts and give us an entrance among them.

Without any seeking on our part, we were brought into touch with at least four anxious souls. An old man found us out, I know not how, and followed me to our boat. I asked him in and inquired his name.

"My name is Dzing," he replied. "But the ques-

tion which distresses me, and to which I can find
no answer, is—What am I to do with my sins?
Our scholars tell us that there is no future state,
but I find it hard to believe them. . . . Oh, sir, I
lie on my bed and think. I sit alone in the day-
time and think. I think and think and think
again, but I cannot tell what is to be done about
my sins. I am seventy-two years of age. I cannot
expect to finish another decade. 'Today knows not
tomorrow's lot,' as the saying is. Can you tell me
what to do with my sins?"

"I can indeed," was my reply. "It is to answer
this very question that we have come so many
thousands of miles. Listen, and I will explain to
you what you want and need to know."

When my companions returned, he heard again
the wonderful story of the Cross, and left us soothed
and comforted . . . glad to know that we had rented
a house and hoped soon tо have Christian colporteurs resident in the city.

Just the same work needed doing in more than
fifty cities in that one province of Chekiang, cities
without any witness for Christ. And oh, the waiting millions beyond! Alone there in his boat, Mr.
Taylor could only cast the burden on the Lord.
Faith was strengthened, and in one of his Bibles
may be seen the entry he made the following day,
January 27, 1874:

Asked God for fifty or a hundred additional native evangelists and as many missionaries as may
be needed to open up the four *Fu's* and forty-eight
Hsien cities still unoccupied in Chekiang, also for

men to break into the nine unoccupied provinces. Asked in the name of Jesus.

I thank Thee, Lord Jesus, for the promise whereon Thou hast given me to rest. Give me all needed strength of body, wisdom of mind, grace of soul to do this Thy so great work.

Yet, strange to say, the immediate sequel was not added strength, but a serious illness. Week after week he lay in helpless suffering, only able to hold on in faith to the heavenly vision. Funds had been so low for months that he had scarcely known how to distribute the little that came in, and there was nothing at all in hand for extension work. But, "we are going on to the interior," he had written to the secretaries in London. "I do so hope to see some of the destitute provinces evangelized before long. I long for it by day and pray for it by night. Can He care less?"

Never had advance seemed more impossible. But in the Bible before him was the record of that transaction of his soul with God, and in his heart was the conviction that, even for inland China, God's time had almost come. And then as he lay there slowly recovering, a letter was put into his hands which had been two months on its way from England. It was from an unknown correspondent.

My dear Sir [the somewhat trembling hand had written], *I bless God*—in two months I hope to place at the disposal of your Council, for further extension of the China Inland Mission work, eight

hundred pounds.[1] Please remember, for *fresh*
provinces. . . .

I think your receipt-form beautiful: "The Lord
our Banner"; "The Lord will provide." If faith
is put forth and praise sent up, I am sure that Je-
hovah of Hosts will honour it.

Eight hundred pounds for "fresh provinces"!
Hardly could the convalescent believe he read aright.
The very secrets of his heart seemed to look back
at him from that sheet of foreign notepaper. Even
before the prayer recorded in his Bible, that letter
had been sent off; and now, just when most needed,
it had reached him with its wonderful confirmation.
Then God's time had surely come!

From his sickroom back to the Yangtze valley was
the next step, and those spring days witnessed a
notable gathering at Chinkiang. There, as in almost all the stations, new life had come to the Chinese Christians. Converts were being received into
the churches, and native leaders were growing in
zeal and usefulness. Older missionaries were encouraged amid the needs of their great districts, and
young men who had made good progress with the
language were eager for pioneering work. As many
as could leave their stations came together for a
week of prayer and conference with Mr. Taylor,
before he and Mr. Judd set out up the great river
to seek a base for the long-prayed-for western branch
of the Mission.

_____

[1]Then equal to about four thousand dollars, gold.

Is it not good of the Lord so to encourage us
[Mr. Taylor wrote from Chinkiang] when we are
sorely tried from want of funds?

For it was not any abundance of supplies that ac-
counted for the new note of joy and hope, as may
be judged from the following letter to a friend
deeply experienced in the life of faith.

Never has our work entailed such real trial or
so much exercise of faith. The sickness of our
beloved friend, Miss Blatchley, and her strong desire to see me; the needs of our dear children; the
state of funds; the changes required in the work
to admit of some going home, others coming out,
and of further expansion, and many other things
not easily expressed in writing, would be crush-
ing burdens if we were to bear them. But the
Lord bears us and them too, and makes our hearts
so very glad in Himself—not Himself plus a bank
balance—that I have never known greater freedom
from care and anxiety.

The other week, when I reached Shanghai, we
were in great and immediate need. The mails
were both in, but no remittance! And the folios
showed no balance at home. I cast the burden on
the Lord. Next morning on waking I felt in-
clined to trouble, but the Lord gave me a word—
"I know their sorrows, and am come down to deliver"; "Certainly I will be with thee"—and be-
for 6 A.M. I was as sure that help was at hand as
when, near noon, I received a letter from Mr.
Mueller which had been to Ningpo and was thus
delayed in reaching me, and which contained more
than three hundred pounds.

My need now is great and urgent, but God is greater and more near. And because *He is* and is *what He is,* all must be, all is, all will be well. Oh, my dear brother, the joy of knowing the living God, of seeing the living God, of resting on the living God in our very special and peculiar circumstances! I am but His agent. He will look after His own honour, provide for His own servants, and supply all our need according to His own riches, you helping by your prayers and work of faith and labour of love.

A note to Mrs. Taylor, of about the same time (April, 1874), breathed a like confidence: "The balance in hand yesterday was eighty-seven cents. The Lord reigns; herein is our joy and rest!" And to Mr. Baller he added, when the balance was still lower, "We have this—and all the promises of God."

"Twenty-five cents," recalled the latter, "*plus* all the promises of God! Why, one felt as rich as Croesus, and sang:

> I would not change my blest estate
> For all the earth holds good or great;
> And while my faith can keep its hold,
> I envy not the sinner's gold."

The hymn of the Conference that spring at Chinkiang was, "In some way or other the Lord will provide," and it was with this in mind that Mr. Taylor wrote to Miss Blatchley:

I am sure that, if we but wait, the Lord *will* provide. . . . We go shortly, that is, Mr. Judd and myself, to see if we can procure headquarters at Wuchang, from which to open up western China as the Lord may enable us. We are urged on to make this effort now, though so weak-handed, both by the need of the unreached provinces and by our having funds in hand for work in them, while we have none for general purposes. . . . I cannot conceive how we shall be helped through next month, though I fully expect we shall be. The Lord cannot and will not fail us.

And yet, at that very time, new difficulties and delays were permitted. Brave and faithful to the last, Miss Blatchley's health had given way under her many responsibilities. The children at Pyrland Road were needing care, and the home work of the Mission was almost at a standstill, for gifted and devoted as she was, matters had tended more and more to come into her hands. Only waiting to establish Mr. Judd at Wuchang, Mr. and Mrs. Taylor hastened home. But even before they could leave China, the beloved friend they hoped to succor had laid all burdens down.

Strange and sorrowful was the homecoming a few weeks later, to find Miss Blatchley's place empty, the children scattered and the weekly prayer meeting discontinued. But even so, the lowest ebb had not been reached. On his way up the Yangtze with Mr. Judd, a fall had seriously injured Mr. Taylor. Concussion of the spine develops slowly, and it was not until he had been at home some weeks that the rush of London life began to tell. Then came gradual paralysis of the lower limbs, completely confining him to his couch. Laid aside in the prime of life, he could only lie in that upstairs room, conscious of all there was to be done, of all that was not being attended to—lie there and rejoice in God.

Yes, rejoice in God! With desires and hopes as limitless as the needs that pressed upon his heart, with the prayer he had prayed and the answers God had given, with opportunities opening in China and a wave of spiritual blessing reviving the churches at home that he longed to see turned into missionary channels, and with little hope, humanly speaking, that he would ever stand or walk again, the deepest thing was joy in the will of God as "good, and acceptable, and perfect." Certain it is that from that place of suffering sprang all the larger growth of the China Inland Mission.

A narrow bed with four posts was the sphere to which Mr. Taylor was now restricted. But between the posts at the foot of the bed—still the map! Yes, there it hung, the map of the whole of China, and round about him day and night was the Presence to which he had access in the name of Jesus. Long after, when prayer had been fully answered and the pioneers of the Mission were preaching Christ far and wide throughout those inland provinces, a leader of the Church of Scotland said to Mr. Taylor:

"You must sometimes be tempted to be proud because of the wonderful way God has used you. I doubt if any man living has had greater honour."

"On the contrary," was the earnest reply, "I often think that God must have been looking for

someone small enough and weak enough for Him
to use, and that He found me."

The outlook did not brighten as the year drew to
a close. Mr. Taylor was less and less able to move,
and could only turn in bed with the help of a rope
fixed above him. At first he had managed to write
a little, but now could not even hold a pen, and circumstances deprived him of Mrs. Taylor's help for
a time. Then it was, with the dawn of 1875, that a
little paper found its way into the Christian press
entitled: *Appeal for Prayer: on behalf of more
than a hundred and fifty millions of Chinese.* Brief-
ly it stated the facts with regard to the nine unevangelized provinces and the aims of the Mission.
Four thousand pounds, it said, had recently been
given for the special purpose of sending the Gospel
to these distant regions. Chinese Christians were
ready to take part in the work. The urgent need
was for more missionaries, young men willing to
face any hardship in leading the way.

"Will each of your Christian readers," it continued, "at once raise his heart to God, spending
one minute in earnest prayer that God will raise
up, this year, eighteen suitable men to devote themselves to this work?"

The appeal did not say that the leader of the
Mission was to all appearance a hopeless invalid.
It did not refer to the fact that the four thousand
pounds had come from his wife and himself, part
of their capital, the whole of which they had consecrated to the work of God. It did not mention the

covenant of two or three years previously, to pray
in faith for the eighteen evangelists until they should
be given. But those who read the little paper felt
there was much behind it, and were moved as men
are not moved by influences that have not their
roots deep in God.

So, before long, Mr. Taylor's correspondence was
largely increased, as was his joy in dealing with it—
or in seeing, rather, how the Lord dealt with it.

The Mission had no paid helpers [he wrote of
this time], but God led volunteers, without pre-
arrangement, to come in from day to day, to write
from dictation. If one who called in the morning
could not stay long enough to answer all letters,
another was sure to come, and perhaps one or two
might look in, in the afternoon. Occasionally a
young friend employed in the city would come in
after business hours and do needful bookkeeping,
or finish letters not already dealt with. So it was
day by day. One of the happiest periods of my
life was that period of forced inactivity, when one
could do nothing but rejoice in the Lord and "wait
patiently" for Him, and see Him meeting all one's
need. Never were my letters, before or since, kept
so regularly and promptly answered.

And the eighteen asked of God began to come.
There was first some correspondence, then they
came to see me in my room. Soon I had a class
studying Chinese at my bedside. In due time the
Lord sent them all forth; and then dear friends
at Mildmay began to pray for my restoration. The
Lord blessed the means used, and I was raised up.

One reason for my being laid aside was gone. Had I been well and able to move about, some might have thought that *my* urgent appeals, rather than God's working, had sent the eighteen men to China. But utterly laid aside, able only to dictate a request for prayer, the answer to our prayers was the more apparent.

Wonderful, too, were the answers to prayer about funds at this time. The monthly remittance to be cabled to China on one occasion was very small, nearly two hundred and thirty-five pounds *less* than the average expenditure to be covered. The matter was brought before the Lord in definite prayer, and in His goodness the answer was not long delayed. That very evening the postman brought a letter which was found to contain a check to be entered, "From the sale of plate"—and the sum was £235.7.9.

Returning from a meeting when able to be about again, Mr. Taylor was accosted by a Russian nobleman who had heard him speak. As they traveled to London together, Count Bobrinsky took out his pocketbook.

"Allow me to give you a trifle," he said, "toward your work in China."

The banknote he handed to Mr. Taylor was for a large sum, and the latter realized that there must be some mistake.

"Did you not mean to give me five pounds?" he questioned; "please let me return this note, it is for fifty!"

"I cannot take it back," replied the Count, no

less surprised. "Five pounds was what I meant to give, but God must have intended you to have fifty. I cannot take it back."

Impressed with what had taken place, Mr. Taylor reached Pyrland Road to find the household gathered for special prayer. A China remittance was to be sent out, and the money in hand was short by £49.11.0. And there upon the table Mr. Taylor laid his banknote for fifty pounds. Could it have come more directly from the Father's hand?

But even with all the answers to prayer of these years, the way was far from open to inland China. Indeed, there came a time, after the eighteen pioneers had been sent out, when it seemed that nothing could prevent war over the murder of a British official. Negotiations had dragged on for months, but the Chinese government would give absolutely no satisfaction, and the British ambassador was on the point of retiring from Peking. It seemed impossible that hostilities could be averted, and there were friends of the Mission who sought to dissuade Mr. Taylor from sailing with a party of eight new workers.

"You will all have to return," they said. "And as to sending off pioneers to the more distant provinces, it is simply out of the question."

Was there some mistake? Had the men and the money been given in vain? Was inland China still to remain closed to the Gospel?

In the third-class cabin of that French steamer there was a man upon his knees, dealing with God.

"My soul yearns, oh how intensely," he had written two years previously, "for the evangelization of the hundred and eighty millions of these unoccupied provinces. Oh, that I had a hundred lives to give or spend for their good!" All that lay in his power he had done, keeping the vision undimmed through every kind of discouragement. And now——?

But God's time had indeed come. With Him it is never "too late." At the last moment, a change came over the Chinese Foreign Office. The Viceroy, Li Hung-chang, hurried to the coast, overtaking the British Minister at Chefoo, and there the memorable Convention was signed which gave liberty of access, at last, to every part of China.

"Just as our brethren were ready," Mr. Taylor delighted to recall, "not too soon and not too late, the long-closed door opened to them of its own accord."

17

WIDER OVERFLOW

Oh, Christ, He is the fountain,
The deep, sweet well of love;
The streams on earth I've tasted,
More deep I'll drink above.
                    —A. R. Cousin

THIRTY THOUSAND MILES the pioneers of the
Mission traveled within the next two years,
throughout the inland provinces of China, everywhere telling the tidings of redeeming love. And
this brought to Mr. Taylor one of the biggest tests
of faith he ever had to meet. For the country
proved wonderfully open, and it was but natural,
after years of hardship in preparing the way, that
the young missionaries should wish to take advantage of suitable openings to establish homes of their
own, from which to work as settled centers. This,
of course, meant homemakers! Several of the pioneers were engaged to be married, and only waited
Mr. Taylor's approval to take the first white women,
as their fellow workers, to the far interior. They
could not foresee, perhaps, as their leader could,

all that would be involved, and that before long
other women would have to take those difficult
journeys, to follow up work begun by busy mothers
in those distant homes.

Years before, however, Mr. Taylor had faced it
all, and had set out on the policy of encouraging
women's work. The outcry was tremendous, as he
knew it would be, when he sanctioned the first departure of married couples to the far interior. Missionary work in China was taking on a new phase;
new sacrifices were called for, new demands were
to be made upon faith and endurance.

But the situation developed gradually. For a year
or more the criticism Mr. Taylor had to face was
directed chiefly against the widespread itinerations
of the pioneers. Not all on these journeys was easy
going. There were dangers and disappointments to
record as well as glorious encouragement. "Without were fightings, within were fears," as of old, and
Mr. Taylor, detained at Chinkiang by the adminis-
trative work of the Mission, was glad to be at hand
to guide and strengthen.

The secret of his own strength was not far to seek.
Whenever work permitted, Mr. Taylor was in the
habit of turning to a little harmonium for refresh-
ment, playing and singing many a favorite hymn,
but always coming back to—

Jesus, I am resting, resting, in the joy of what
Thou art; I am finding out the greatness of Thy
loving heart.

One of the eighteen evangelists, Mr. George Nichol, was with him on one occasion when some letters were handed in to his office, bringing news of serious rioting in two of the older stations of the Mission. Thinking that Mr. Taylor might wish to be alone, the younger man was about to withdraw when, to his surprise, someone began to whistle. It was the soft refrain of the same well-loved hymn:

Jesus, I am resting, resting, in the joy of what Thou art . . .

Turning back, Mr. Nichol could not help exclaiming, "How *can* you whistle, when our friends are in so much danger!"

"Would you have me anxious and troubled?" was the quiet reply. "That would not help them, and would certainly incapacitate me for my work. I have just to roll the burden on the Lord."

Day and night this was his secret, "just to roll the burden on the Lord." Frequently those who were wakeful in the little house at Chinkiang might hear, at two or three in the morning, the soft refrain of Mr. Taylor's favorite hymn. He had learned that, for him, only one life was possible—just that blessed life of resting and rejoicing in the Lord under all circumstances, while He dealt with the difficulties, inward and outward, great and small.

* * * * *

Mr. Taylor was at home again in London. Six millions of people in North China were facing starvation, in a province in which there were no missionaries save a few Inland Mission pioneers.

Children were dying in thousands and young girls being sold into slavery and carried away in troops to cities farther south. Mr. Taylor had come home burdened with the awful condition and was doing all in his power to forward relief work. Funds were available for the rescue of children, but where was the woman who could go to that stricken province to undertake the work? No white woman had ever been beyond the mountains that separated Shansi from the coast, and to get there meant a two weeks' journey by mule-litter, over dangerous roads, with miserable inns at night.

Yet it was for this undertaking that Mr. and Mrs. Taylor separated when he had been home only a few months. A little worn notebook recalls the experiences through which her faith was strengthened as she waited upon God to know whether or not the call was really from Him. But once she did know, not even the sacrifice involved for Mr. Taylor, whose suggestion it had been, held her back. Two little ones of her own, four older children and an adopted daughter made a young family of seven to leave behind. How were they to be cared for? All her hard questions she brought to God, and He not only answered them, meeting every need as it arose, but gave grace for the parting and all the difficult, dangerous work in China.

> Cross-loving men are needed [Mr. Taylor had written before coming home]. Oh, may God make you and me of this spirit. . . . I feel so ashamed that you and the dear children should affect me

more than millions here who are perishing—while
we are sure of eternity together.

After that, it was easier for Mr. Taylor to let other
women join the front ranks, when his own wife had
led the way. And part of his reward when they were
reunited, a year later (1879) was to have her with
him in China as, in province after province of the
interior, women's work quietly opened up.

Fascinating and heart-moving as any novel is the
story of those years. Wrecked in the Yangtze gorges,
the first women who went to the far west spent a
strange Christmas amid their bridal belongings
spread out to dry upon the rocks. And what crowds
overwhelmed them upon arrival at their destina-
tions!

"For nearly two months past," Mrs. Nichol wrote
from Chungking, "I have seen some hundreds of
women daily. Our house has been like a fair."

More than once she fainted from weariness in the
midst of her guests—the only white woman in a
province of some sixty millions of people—returning to consciousness to find the women fanning her,
full of affection and concern. One lady, who cared
for her like a mother, would send round her own
sedan chair with an urgent request for Mrs. Nichol
to return in it immediately. The most comfortable
bed in her own apartment was waiting, and sending
out all the younger women she would sit down herself to fan the weary visitor till she fell asleep. Then
an inviting dinner was prepared, and on no account

was Mrs. Nichol allowed to leave until she had made a proper meal.

That was the surprise that everywhere awaited the first women who went—the people were glad to see them, were eager often, to hear their message, showing not only natural curiosity but real heart sympathy. And how soon it began to tell—this living and preaching Christ so openly! By the end of the second year after missionary women came on the scene, the pioneers were rejoicing in sixty or seventy converts gathered into little churches in the far inland provinces.

First to go to the women of the Northwest, three months' journey up the Han River, Emily King was the first also to be called Home (May, 1881). But before her brief course ended, she had the joy of seeing no fewer than eighteen women baptized in confession of their faith in Christ. Dying of typhoid fever in the city of Hanchung, this it was that raised her above the grief of leaving her husband desolate and their little one motherless. The Man of Sorrows was seeing of "the travail of his soul" among those for whom He had waited long— and she, too, was satisfied.

No one undertsood better than Mr. Taylor the cost at which such work was done; no one followed it with more unfailing prayer.

I cannot tell you how glad my heart is [he wrote to his mother in the midst of much trial] to see the work extending and consolidating in the re-

mote parts of China. It is worth living for and
worth dying for.

After that, developments were rapid and wonderful. But associated with every fresh advance, every
access of power and blessing, there was in Mr. Taylor's own experience a corresponding period of suffering and trial. Deeper down, deeper down that
life had to go, in God. Outwardly it might seem,
at times, that the work was carried on a floodtide of
success. Glorious steps of faith were taken; glorious
answers to prayer were received. But the preparation of heart beforehand and the steady burden-
bearing afterwards were known only to those who
shared them behind the scenes. One stands silenced
before such profound heart-searchings, such trials
of faith, such exercise of soul. Given a man prepared to go all lengths with God, prepared to die
daily in quiet, practical reality, prepared to be the
servant of his brethren (least of all and servant of
all), prepared to stand for them in ceaseless inter-
cession, not only bearing with their failures and
weaknesses, but bearing them up in creative faith
and love that lift to higher levels—thus and thus
only is such spiritual success possible.

Before the forward movement which had brought
new life to the work—when women missionaries first
went inland—there had been a period of intense and
prolonged suffering. Three times over in 1879 Mr.
Taylor's life was in danger through serious sick-
nesses, and in the year that followed, while the new
line of things was being tested and established by

God's blessing, the Mission was faced with intense
and accumulated trials. Mrs. Taylor touched upon
a deep principle when she wrote at that time:

> Don't you think that if we set ourselves not to
> allow any pressure to rob us of communion with
> the Lord, we may live lives of hourly triumph,
> the echo of which will come back to us from every
> part of the Mission? I have been feeling these
> last months that of all our work the most impor-
> tant is that unseen, upon the mount of intercession.
> *Our* faith must gain the victory for the fellow-
> workers God has given us. They fight the seen and
> we must fight the unseen battle. And dare we
> claim less than constant victory, when it is for
> *Him,* and we come in His Name?

But times of trial, as by a spiritual law, always
led on to enlargement and blessing. It was so, for
example, when, after parting from Mrs. Taylor who
could no longer be spared from home, the leader
of the Mission set his face westward for conference
with some of the younger workers.

> You are ploughing the Mediterranean [he wrote]
> and will soon see Naples. . . . I am waiting for a
> steamer to Wuchang. I need not, cannot tell you
> how much I miss you, but God is making me feel
> how rich we are in His presence and love. . . .
> He is helping me to rejoice in our adverse circum-
> stances, in our poverty, in the retirements from our
> Mission. All these difficulties are only platforms
> for the manifestation of His grace, power and love.

> I am very busy [he continued from Wuchang
> when the meetings had begun]. God is giving us

a happy time of fellowship together, *and is con-
firming us in the principles on which we are acting.*

That one brief sentence, taken in connection with
the crisis to which they had come, lets in a flood of
light upon the important sequel to those days of
fellowship at Wuchang. For unconsciously to the
younger missionaries, it was a crisis, and more was
hanging in the balance than Mr. Taylor himself
could realize. After years of prayer and patient,
persevering effort, a position of unparalleled opportunity had been reached. Inland China lay open
before them. At all the settled stations in the far
north, south and west, reinforcements were needed.
Not to advance would be to retreat from the position of faith taken up at the beginning. It would
be to look at difficulties rather than at the living
God. True, funds were low, had been for years,
and the new workers coming out were few. It
would have been easy to say, "For the present, no
further extension is possible." But *not* to go forward would be to cripple and hinder the work; to
throw away opportunities God had given, and before long to close stations opened at great cost. This,
surely, could not be His way for the evangelization
of inland China.

What then was the outcome of those days of quiet
waiting upon God? It was a step of faith so startling that, for a time, the sympathy of friends at
home seemed doubtful. For it was no less than an
appeal to the home churches—later on signed by almost all the members of the Mission—for *seventy*

new workers to be sent out within the next three years. The entire membership of the Mission numbered barely a hundred, and funds had long been straitened. Yet, so sure was the group at Wuchang of being guided of God in their definite prayer and expectation that one of them exclaimed:

"If only we could meet again and have a united praise meeting, when the last of The Seventy have reached China!"

Three years had been agreed upon as the period in which the answer should be looked for (1882-84), as it would hardly be possible to receive and arrange for so many new workers in a shorter time.

"We shall be widely scattered then," said another, of a practical turn of mind. "But why not have the praise meeting now? Why not give thanks for The Seventy before we separate?"

This was approved and the meeting held, so that all who had joined in the prayer united also in the thanksgiving.

And The Seventy *were* given, wonderfully given, in the next three years. But faith was thrown into the crucible in many ways. Trial as to funds continued to be serious, but was surpassed by trial connected with the work itself. And yet Mr. Taylor was able to write:

I do feel more and more the blessedness of real trust in God. Faith, He tries, but sustains. And when our faithfulness fails, His remains unshaken. "He cannot deny himself." . . .

The Lord Jesus, this year of very peculiar trial

from almost every quarter, does make my heart
well up and overflow with His love. He knows
what separations and other incidents of our service
mean, and He so wonderfully makes all loss to be
gain! . . . Excuse my running on in this way. My
glad heart seems as if it must have vent, even
among figures and remittances.

As the first of the three years wore on, years in
which The Seventy were looked for, it became evident that there was serious misgiving at home as
to the appeal. Mr. Taylor was at Chefoo at the
time, and felt it laid on his heart to ask the Lord
to put His seal on the matter in a way that could
not be mistaken. It was at one of the daily prayer
meetings, on or about the second of February, and
the few who were present were conscious of much
liberty in laying this request before God.

We knew that our Father loves to please His
children, and we asked Him lovingly to please us,
as well as to encourage timid ones at home, by
leading some one of His wealthy stewards to make
room for large blessing *for himself and his family*
by giving liberally to this special object.

A few days later Mr. Taylor sailed for England
and it was not until he stopped at Aden that he
learned the result. No account of that special
prayer meeting had been sent home; but at Pyrland
Road they had had the joy of receiving *on the
second of February,* a sum of three thousand pounds,
with the words: "Ask of me, and I shall give thee
the heathen for thine inheritance, and the uttermost

parts of the earth for thy possession." Nor was this
all. The gift was sent in an unusual way. the names
of *five children* being added to those of the parents.
What could have been more encouraging than to see
how literally God answered prayer?

It was the same some years later, when another
great step forward was taken in faith.

God had so blessed with the going out of The
Seventy that the Mission had been lifted on to a
new plane of influence at home. During those years
something of the pioneering character of the work
had become known. "They are opening up the
country," wrote Alexander Wylie of the London
Missionary Society, "and this is what we want. Other
missions are doing a good work, but they are not
doing *this* work." So that, when John McCarthy
reached England, after walking clear across China,
from east to west, preaching Christ all the way;
when J. W. Stevenson and Dr. Henry Soltau came
home, the first to enter western China from Burma,
following the Yangtze to Shanghai; and when they
were joined in England by Mr. Taylor with the
appeal of the Mission for seventy new workers,
Christian hearts were deeply stirred. The way had
been prepared by the devoted labors of Mr. Taylor's brother-in-law, Mr. Benjamin Broomhall, who
for seven years had represented the Mission in London, and who with Mrs. Broomhall made its headquarters at Pyrland Road a center of love and prayer.
With a genius for friendship and a heart to embrace
the whole Church of God, Mr. Broomhall found

openings in many directions for the testimony of the Mission; for people were keen to hear how the seemingly impossible had been brought to pass, and how without appeals for money, or even collections, the growing work was sustained.

If you are not dead yet [was the charming communication of a child at Cambridge to whom "Hudson Taylor" was a household word] I want to send you the money I have saved up to help the little boys and girls of China to love Jesus.

Will you do me the kindness [urged Canon Wilberforce of Southampton] to give a Bible-reading in my house to about sixty people . . . and spend the night with us? *Please* do us this favour, in the Master's name.

Much love to you in the Lord [wrote Lord Radstock from the Continent]. You are a great help to us in England by strengthening our faith.

From Dr. Andrew Bonar came a hundred pounds forwarded from an unknown Presbyterian friend "who cares for the land of Sinim." Spurgeon sent his characteristic invitations to the Tabernacle, and Miss Macpherson to Bethnal Green.

My heart is still in the glorious work [wrote Mr. Berger with a check for five hundred pounds]. Most heartily do I join you in praying for seventy more labourers—but do not stop at seventy! Surely we shall see greater things than these, if we are empty of self, seeking only God's glory and the salvation of souls.

And Mr. Berger's faith was justified: "Surely we shall see greater things than these." The Seventy as God gave them proved to be an overflowing answer to prayer. Before the last party sailed, they had been overtaken by the well-known "Cambridge Band," whose consecrated testimony before they left England swept the British universities with a profound spiritual movement which reached on and out to the ends of the earth. It was a rising tide indeed of spiritual blessing, and the new edition Mr. Taylor found time to publish of *China's Spiritual Need and Claims* deepened and continued the work.

Before the Cambridge party could sail, detained as they were by revival in university centers, Mr. Taylor went on ahead to China, missing the final farewell meeting at Exeter Hall. The contrast could hardly have been more marked between the enthusiasm of that great gathering for all the Mission stood for and the solitary man alone upon his knees, day after day, in the cabin of the ship that was carrying him back to the stern realities of the fight. "Borne on a great wave of fervent enthusiasm," as the editorial secretary of the Church Missionary Society expressed it, the work had been swept into a new place in the sympathy and confidence of the Lord's people. "The Mission has become popular," Mr. Broomhall was writing, not without concern. But out in China, Hudson Taylor had to face the other side of that experience.

Soon we shall be in the midst of the battle [he wrote from the China Sea], but the Lord our God in the midst of us is mighty—so we will trust and

not be afraid. "He will save." He will save all
the time and in everything.

And again, some months later:

Flesh and heart often fail: let them fail! He
faileth not. Pray very much, pray constantly, for
Satan rages against us. . . .

There is much to distress. Your absence is a great
and ever-present trial, and there is all the ordinary
and extraordinary conflict. But the encourage-
ments are also wonderful—no other word approach-
es the truth, and half of them cannot be told in
writing. No one dreams of the mighty work going on in connection with our Mission. Other
missions too, doubtless, are being greatly used. I
look for a wonderful year.

And a wonderful year it was (1886), leading up
to the next forward movement with its outstanding
answers to prayer alluded to above.

Mr. Taylor had spent several months inland, visiting districts in which many of the new workers
were located. He had traveled through Shansi,
holding conferences which were reported in a
precious little book entitled, *Days of Blessing*. The
quiet power of his life and testimony opened up to
younger workers the deep things of God. "Days
of Blessing" they were indeed, especially in Pastor
Hsi's district, when Mr. Taylor met the converted
Confucian scholar for the first time. Their mutual
love and appreciation it was beautiful to see, as
they conferred together about the future of the
work.

"We all saw visions at that time," recalled Mr. Stevenson who was with them. "Those were days of Heaven upon earth. Nothing seemed difficult."

Coming down the river Han on the last stage of this journey, it was quite natural for Mr. Taylor to take charge of a little girl five years of age, whose missionary parents realized that only a change to the coast could save the child's life. There was no woman in the party, and they knew that for a month or six weeks little Annie would have no one to care for her, day or night, save the Director of the Mission. But they were more than satisfied.

My little charge is wonderfully improving [he was able to write from the boat]. She clings to me very lovingly, and it is sweet to feel little arms about one's neck once more.

Straight from this journey, Mr. Taylor came to the first meeting of the China Council of the Mission, as the year drew to a close. The newly appointed superintendents of the provinces gathered at Anking, including Mr. Stevenson and Mr. McCarthy, and a whole week was given to prayer and fasting, so that with prepared hearts they might face the important issues before them. With wisdom born of twenty years' experience as Director of the work Mr. Taylor sought to lead to wise and helpful organization with a view to larger developments, but even he was startled by the suggestion that grew out of the conference—that for anything like advance, *a hundred new workers* were urgently needed.

Very carefully the situation was gone over, and

Mr. Taylor had at last to agree that with fifty
central stations and China open before them from
end to end, a hundred new workers in the following year would be all too few for hoped-for developments.   Mr. Stevenson, by this time Deputy Director of the Mission, was full of faith and courage.
He sent out a little slip, explaining the situation
to all the members of the Mission, and cabled to
London with Mr. Taylor's permission—"Praying for
a hundred new workers in 1887."

But what a thrill that meant at home! *A hundred new recruits for China in one year?* No Mission in existence had ever dreamed of sending out
reinforcements on such a scale. The China Inland
Mission then numbered only a hundred and ninety
members; and to pray for a more than fifty per cent
increase within the next twelve months—well, people almost held their breath! but only until Mr.
Taylor came home. "Strong in faith, giving glory
to God," he brought a spiritual uplift that was soon
felt throughout the fellowship of the Mission. The
three-fold prayer they were praying in China was
taken up by countless hearts: that God would give
the hundred workers, those of His own choice; that
He would supply the fifty thousand dollars of extra
income needed, no appeal or collections being made;
and that the money might come in in *large* sums,
to keep down correspondence, a practical point with
a small office staff.

And what happened in 1887? Six hundred men
and women actually offered to the Mission in that

year, of whom *one hundred and two* were chosen,
equipped and sent out. Not fifty but *fifty-five* thousand dollars extra were actually received, without
solicitation, so that every need was met. And how
many letters had to be written and receipts made
out to acknowledge this large sum? Just *eleven gifts*
covered it all, scarcely adding appreciably to the
work of the staff, taxed to the utmost in other ways.
And best of all, faith was strengthened and hearts
were stirred with new and deeper longings wherever
the story of "The Hundred" became known.

One unexpected result was a visit to London of
a young American businessman, who was also an
evangelist, upon whose heart it had been laid to
invite Mr. Taylor to come to the States. Mr. Henry
W. Frost was so sure that his visit to England for
this purpose had been guided of God that the disappointment when Mr. Taylor did not respond was
overwhelming. Drawn to the Inland Mission by all
he had seen and heard, and to Mr. Taylor in particular, it was in much perplexity he returned to New
York, feeling that his mission had been in vain. But
God's working in the matter had only just begun.

Mr. Taylor did come to America the following
summer (1888) and was cordially received by D. L.
Moody and the leaders of the Niagara Bible Conference among others. There and at Northfield surprising developments took place in answer to prayer
—chiefly the prayers that went up from the heart
that had known such disappointment and was now

rejoicing to see the hand of God working far beyond anything he had asked or thought.

For when Mr. Taylor went on to China, three
months later, he did not go alone. Fourteen young
men and women accompanied him, a precious gift
of God to the Mission from this great continent.
Various denominations were represented, both from
the States and Canada, and the gifts and prayers so
unexpectedly called forth were but the beginning
of a steady stream which has flowed out for China
ever since. So great was the interest that a North
American Council had to be formed, and at no little sacrifice to himself and his family, Mr. Henry
W. Frost, whom God had used to bring it all to
pass, undertook to represent and guide the work.
It was one of the most fruitful developments to
which the Lord ever led in connection with Mr.
Taylor's ministry, and filled with new faith and
courage he went on to meet all that was to grow
out of it.

For a great step forward had been taken, and
from that time onward the China Inland Mission
which had always been interdenominational became
international. Twelve years remained of the active
service of Mr. Taylor's life, and they were years
of world-wide ministry. A visit to Scandinavia
opened to him the warm hearts of Swedish and
Norwegian Christians; Germany sent devoted con-
tingents to work in association with the Mission;
Australia and New Zealand welcomed Mr. Taylor
as one long known and loved, and the China Coun-

cil in Shanghai became the center of a greater organization than its founder had ever imagined.

The spiritual overflow of those last years was best of all—just the same streams of blessing, only reaching now to the ends of the earth. The impressions of an Episcopalian minister who was Mr. Taylor's host in Melbourne are interesting in this connection.

He was an object lesson in quietness. He drew from the bank of heaven every farthing of his daily income—"My peace I give unto you." Whatever did not agitate the Saviour or ruffle His spirit, was not to agitate him. The serenity of the Lord Jesus concerning any matter, and at its most critical moment, was his ideal and practical possession. He knew nothing of rush or hurry, or quivering nerves or vexation of spirit. He knew that there is a peace passing all understanding, and that he could not do without it. . . .

"I am in the study, you are in the big spareroom," I said to Mr. Taylor at length. "You are occupied with millions, I with tens. Your letters are pressingly important, mine of comparatively little moment. Yet I am worried and distressed, while you are always calm. Do tell me what makes the difference."

"My dear Macartney," he replied, "the peace you speak of is, in my case, more than a delightful privilege, it is a necessity. I could not possibly get through the work I have to do without the peace of God 'which passeth all understanding' keeping my heart and mind."

That was my chief experience of Mr. Taylor.

Are you in a hurry, flurried, distressed? Look up! See the Man in the glory! Let the face of Jesus shine upon you—the wonderful face of the Lord Jesus Christ. Is He worried or distressed? There is no care on His brow, no least shade of anxiety. Yet the affairs are His as much as yours.

"Keswick teaching," as it is called, was not new to me. I had received those glorious truths and was preaching them to others. But here was *the real thing*, an embodiment of "Keswick teaching" such as I had never hoped to see. It impressed me profoundly. Here was a man almost sixty years of age, bearing tremendous burdens, yet absolutely calm and untroubled. Oh, the pile of letters! any one of which might contain news of death, of lack of funds, of riots or serious trouble. Yet all were opened, read and answered with the same tranquillity—Christ his reason for peace, his power for calm. Dwelling in Christ, he drew upon His very being and resources, in the midst of and concerning the matters in question. And this he did by an attitude of faith as simple as it was continuous.

Yet he was delightfully free and natural. I can find no words to describe it save the Scriptural expression "in God." He was in God all the time and God in him. It was that true "abiding" of John fifteen. But oh, the lover-like attitude that underlay it! He had in relation to Christ a most bountiful experience of the Song of Solomon. It was a wonderful combination—the strength and tenderness of one who, amid stern preoccupation, like that of a judge on the bench, carried in his heart the light and love of home.

And through it all, the vision and spiritual urgency of earlier years remained unchanged. Indeed the sense of responsibility to obey the last command of the Lord Jesus Christ only increased, as he came to see more clearly the meaning of the great commission.

I confess with shame [he wrote as late as 1889] that the question, what did our Lord *really mean* by His command to "preach the gospel to every creature" had never been raised by me. I had laboured for many years to carry the Gospel further afield, as have many others; had laid plans for reaching every unevangelized province and many smaller districts in China, without realizing the plain meaning of our Saviour's words.

"To every creature"? And the total number of Protestant communicants in China was but forty thousand. Double that number, treble it, to include adherents, and suppose each one to be a messenger of light to eight of his own people—and, even so, only one million would be reached. *"To every creature"*: the words burned into his very soul. But how far was the Church, how far had he been himself from taking them literally, as intended to be acted upon!

How are we going to treat the Lord Jesus Christ [he wrote under deep conviction] with regard to this last command? Shall we definitely drop the title "Lord" as applied to Him? Shall we take the ground that we are quite willing to recognize Him as our Saviour, as far as the penalty of sin is concerned, but are not prepared to own ourselves "bought with a price," or Christ as having claim to our unquestioning obedience? . . .

How few of the Lord's people have practically recognized the truth that Christ is either *Lord of all* or He is *not Lord at all!* If we can judge God's Word, instead of being judged by it, if we can give God as much or as little as we like, then we are lords and He the indebted one, to be grateful for our dole and obliged by our compliance with His wishes. If on the other hand He is Lord, let us treat Him as such. "Why call ye me, Lord, Lord, and do not the things which I say?"

So, all unexpectedly, Hudson Taylor came to the widest outlook of his life, the purpose which was to dominate the closing years of its active leadership: nothing less than a definite, systematic effort to do just what the Master commanded; to carry the glad tidings of His redeeming love to every man, woman and child throughout the whole of China. He did not think that the China Inland Mission could do it all. But he did believe that with proper division of the field the missionary forces of the Church were well equal to the task.

* * * * *

But he was not to see it in his day. With the willing co-operation of the Mission, a beginning was made in Kiangsi, and plans were maturing for advance all over the field. But in the providence of God a deep baptism of suffering had to come first. The Boxer madness of 1900 swept the country, and the Inland Mission was more exposed to its fury than any other. Mr. Taylor had just reached England after a serious breakdown in health, and under a feeling of concern that she hardly understood, Mrs. Taylor persuaded him to go on to a quiet spot in Switzerland where his health had been restored some years previously.

And there it was the blow fell, and telegram after telegram came telling of riots, massacres, and the hunting down of refugees in station after station of the Mission—until the heart that so long had upheld these beloved fellow-workers before the Lord could endure no more and almost ceased to beat. But for the protection of that remote valley (Davos) where news could in measure be kept from him, Hudson Taylor would have been himself among those whose lives were laid down for Christ's sake and for China in the oversweeping horror of that summer. As it was, he lived through it, holding on to God.

"I cannot read," he said when things were at their worst; "I cannot pray, I can scarcely even think — but I can trust."

*   *   *   *   *

The Boxer crisis passed and the calm words of a white-haired pastor in Shansi came true:

"Kingdoms may perish," he said, almost with his last breath, "but the Church of Christ can never be destroyed."

In this confidence, he and hundreds of other Chinese Christians sealed their testimony with their blood; and in this confidence the witness of faithful lives that had been spared began again.

Mr. D. E. Hoste, whom Mr. Taylor had appointed as his successor, was enabled to deal so wisely with the situation that enemies were turned to friends and the Chinese authorities were not slow to express their appreciation of a literal carrying out of the commands of Christ which meant more, from their point of view, than all the preaching that had gone before.

And Mr. Taylor lived to see the new day of opportunity opening in China; lived to return to the land of his love and prayers. But he returned alone. The beloved companion of many years, who had so brightened the closing days of their pilgrimage together, rests above Vevey, by the Lake of Geneva, where they made their last home. With his son and daughter-in-law—the present writers—he turned his face once more toward China, and at seventy-three years of age made one of the most remarkable itinerations of his lifetime.

How the Christians loved and revered him as he passed from station to station, everywhere welcomed as "China's Benefactor," the one through whom the Gospel had reached those inland provinces! After traveling up the Yangtze to Hankow and spending some weeks in the northern province of Honan, Mr. Taylor was strengthened to undertake one more journey. Little had he ever expected to find himself in Hunan. First of the nine unevangelized provinces to be entered by pioneers of the C.I.M., it had proved by far the most difficult. Adam Dorward, after more than eight years of toil and suffering—homeless, persecuted, escaping from a riot to die alone at last—had rejoiced to give his life in hope of the results we see today. For more than thirty years Mr. Taylor had borne that province upon his heart in prayer, and it was fitting that the last rich joy to come to him should be the loving welcome of Hunan converts. Eagerly the Christians gathered at the capital, in the home of Dr. Frank Keller—first to obtain permanent residence in the province—looking forward to the services of Sunday with the beloved leader of whom they had heard so much. Those who had come in early enough, met him on Saturday, when also the missionaries in the city attended the reception hospitably planned by Dr. and Mrs. Keller.

* * * * *

But it was that evening the call came. No, it was hardly death—just the glad, swift entry upon life eternal.

"My father, my father, the chariot of Israel, and the horsemen thereof!"

And the very room seemed filled with unutterable peace.

18

STREAMS FLOWING STILL

He told me of a river bright
    That flows from Him to me,
That I might be, for His delight,
    A fair and fruitful tree.
               —TERSTEEGEN

WHEN MR. TAYLOR was caught away from the heart of China—passing in one painless moment to the presence of the Lord he loved—a feeling almost of suspense held many hearts. What will become of the Mission now? was the unspoken question. Hudson Taylor was a man of such unusual faith! It was all right while he lived and prayed. But now—? The thought was natural, but years have only proved that though the father and long-loved leader of the work passed on, the God in whom was all his confidence remains.

The lines at the head of this chapter were dear to Mr. Taylor, and express the essence of his spiritual secret.

It is very simple [he wrote] but has He not planted us by the river of living water that we may be, *for His delight,* fair and fruitful to His people?

God was first in Hudson Taylor's life—not the work, not the needs of China or of the Mission, not his own experiences. He knew that the promise was true, "Delight thyself also in the Lord; and he shall give thee the desires of thine heart." And is the promise less true for us today? Let the experience of one of the leaders of the Mission stand for the many.

> The work is always increasing [Miss Soltau wrote], and were it not for the consciousness of Christ as my life, hour by hour, I could not go on. But He is teaching me glorious lessons of His sufficiency, and each day I am carried forward with no feeling of strain or fear of collapse.

Streams flowing still—how true it has been in the experience of the enlarged and ever-growing Mission! The main facts as to the developments of the last thirty years are given in an appendix, and wonderful facts they are. But here we would only refer —as we turn from the past to the present—to the practical side of Mr. Taylor's spiritual life. He knew that the thought expressed by one deeply versed in the things of God is true: "God does not give us overcoming life: He gives us life *as we overcome.*"[1] To him, the secret of overcoming lay in daily, hourly fellowship with God; and this, he found, could only be maintained by secret prayer

---

[1] See *My Utmost for His Highest,* by Oswald Chambers, page 47.

and feeding upon the Word through which **He reveals** Himself to the waiting soul.

It was not easy for Mr. Taylor, in his changeful life, to make time for prayer and Bible study, but he knew that it was vital. Well do the writers remember traveling with him month after month in northern China, by cart and wheelbarrow, with the poorest of inns at night. Often with only one large room for coolies and travelers alike, they would screen off a corner for their father and another for themselves, with curtains of some sort; and then, after sleep at last had brought a measure of quiet, they would hear a match struck and see the flicker of candlelight which told that Mr. Taylor, however weary, was poring over the little Bible in two volumes always at hand. From two to four A. M. was the time he usually gave to prayer; the time when he could be most sure of being undisturbed to wait upon God. That flicker of candlelight has meant more to them than all they have read or heard on secret prayer; it meant reality, not preaching but practice.

The hardest part of a missionary career, Mr. Taylor found, is to maintain regular, prayerful Bible study. "Satan will always find you something to do," he would say, "when you ought to be occupied about that, if it is only arranging a window blind." Fully would he have endorsed the weighty words:

Take time. Give God time to reveal Himself to you. Give yourself time to be silent and quiet before Him, waiting to receive, through the Spirit, the assurance of His presence with you, His power working in you. Take time to read His Word as in His presence, that from it you may know what He asks of you and what He promises you. Let the Word create around you, create within you a holy atmosphere, a holy heavenly light, in which your soul will be refreshed and strengthened for the work of daily life.[2]

It was just because he did this that Hudson Taylor's life was full of joy and power, by the grace of God. When over seventy years of age he paused, Bible in hand, as he crossed the sitting-room in Lausanne, and said to one of his children: "I have just finished reading the Bible through, today, for the fortieth time in forty years." And he not only read it, he lived it.

Hudson Taylor stopped at no sacrifice in following Christ. "Cross-loving men are needed," he wrote in the midst of his labors in China, and if he could speak to us today would it not be to call us to that highest of all ambitions: "that I may know him [the One we, too, supremely love], and the power of his resurrection and the fellowship of his sufferings." Can we not hear again the tones of his quiet voice as he says:

There is a needs-be for us to give ourselves for the life of the world. An easy, non-self-denying life will never be one of power. Fruit-bearing in-

---

2Rev. Andrew Murray, in *The Secret of Adoration*, from the Introduction.

volves cross-bearing. There are not two Christs—
an easy-going one for easy-going Christians, and a
suffering, toiling one for exceptional believers.
There is only one Christ. Are you willing to abide
in *Him,* and thus to bear much fruit?

APPENDIX

WHEN MR. HUDSON TAYLOR laid down the leadership of the Mission in 1900, five years before his Home-call, the China Inland Mission numbered 750 missionaries. Today (1932) its membership is 1,285. The income while Mr. Taylor was directing the work and sustaining it with his prayers ran into millions of dollars, unasked save of God—no less than four million dollars. The total income since 1900 has been almost twenty million dollars, unasked save of God. And there has been and is no debt. Seven hundred Chinese workers were connected with the Mission, rich answer to Mr. Taylor's prayers, and the converts baptized from the commencement numbered thirteen thousand. Today there are between three and four thousand Chinese workers connected with the C. I. M., and the baptisms since 1900 alone number a hundred thousand. "Not unto us, O Lord, not unto us, but unto thy name give glory."

Mr. Taylor was unique in his relation to the work, of which he was founder as well as Director:

no one in this sense could take his place. Yet, in the leader God raised up to follow him, a gift no less unique has been given. Bearing responsibilities greatly increased since 1900, Mr. D. E. Hoste has been sustained in a prayer-life which is the benediction of the Mission, while under his guidance, through years of storm and stress, the work has gone steadily on from strength to strength.

True, there have been times of overwhelming trial and apparent setback. When the revolution broke out and China, almost overnight, became a republic, a reign of terror prevailed in certain districts and the Mission was again called to add to its martyr roll. In the city of Sian, once capital of the empire, Mrs. Beckman and six children of missionary families were murdered by a lawless mob, also Mr. Vatne who was trying to protect them. Not a few missionaries were obliged to leave their stations for places of greater safety; others, who held on, were enabled to protect many of the terrified people round them, women especially, who fled to the missionary homes for refuge. Precious opportunities were afforded in those days for living as well as preaching the Gospel, and the friendly feeling toward missionaries in the interior was very marked.

With the spread of lawlessness and cruel banditry, as well as the organized agitation among students, missionaries and Chinese Christians alike have had to face great and increasing dangers. But the amazing thing has really been that changes so stupendous could take place without more bloodshed and upheaval. Swept away from all the old moorings, reaching out with passionate desire for better things, China in her helplessness has fallen among thieves. The desperate counsels of Communism and Bolshevism have prevailed in many places, to the unspeakable aggravation of existing evils, and latterly the relentless aggressions of neighboring powers have added to the distresses of the situation.

"When brothers fall out," the old Chinese proverb has it, "then strangers are apt to take advantage of them"; again, "to complete a thing, a hundred years is not sufficient; to destroy, one day is more than enough."

Yet in the midst of it all, the protecting hand of God has been over the work, so that advance has been steady in connection with the evangelistic program of the Inland Mission. The fact that the work *is* evangelistic rather than institutional accounts for much of the friendliness of the people and their readiness to listen to the consolations of the Gospel. Never have there been such opportunities as there are today for the sale of Christian literature and the witness of loving hearts to the saving power of Christ. "The healing of His seamless dress" is the healing that China needs, and many are the wounded hearts turning to Him for life and hope amid conditions of despair.

That such an hour is no time for retrenchment in the missionary enterprise must be manifest to all who look to God, who "look up," rather than at circumstances. This it is that has called the China

Inland Mission, of recent years, out from a policy
of waiting, into a glorious advance along the lines
of Mr. Taylor's latest and greatest vision. With regard to the fresh realization that came to him of
the Lord's plain meaning in His definite commission, "Preach the gospel to every creature," Mr.
Taylor had written:

> This work will not be done without crucifixion,
> without consecration which is prepared *at any cost*
> to carry out the Master's command. But given that,
> I believe in my inmost soul that it will be done.

> If ever in my life I was conscious of being led of
> God, it was in the writing and publication of those
> papers [*To Every Creature*].

Living seed, though it fall into the ground and
die, will yet bring forth fruit. Mr. Taylor had long
gone to his reward when a second baptism of suffering was permitted, five years ago, in the overwhelming distress of 1927. More than six hundred
members of the Mission were obliged to evacuate
their stations in that tragic year, when Western Gov-
ernments, alarmed at a new and fierce outbreak of
anti-foreign agitation, ordered their nationals to
withdraw from the interior.

This was inspired by propagandists from Moscow
[as Dr. Robert H. Glover,[1] now the North American
Director of the Mission, writes] who incited the

---

[1]The Rev. Robert Hall Glover, M.D. assumed, at the close
of 1929, the responsibilities which the Rev. Henry W. Frost,
D.D. laid down after forty-two years of devoted and successful leadership. Dr. Frost, to the thankfulness of all concerned, continues his invaluable connection with the Mission
as Home Director Emeritus.

Chinese soldiery and student body to acts of violence, particularly directed against missionaries and other foreigners. . . . And so the large majority of missionaries all over China were forced to leave their stations, their beloved converts and the work of years, and make their way to the coast. Thus, almost before they were aware of it, several hundred C. I. M. missionaries, among others, found themselves out of inland China, with the door closed behind them.

To provide for these refugees in the overcrowded settlements imposed a heavy burden on the funds of the Mission. Fourteen houses had to be rented in Shanghai alone, and furnished in some sort, and all the traveling expenses had to be met out of straitened resources. For many supporters of the Mission at home, seeing that the work was for the time being largely at a standstill, found other channels for their missionary giving, and had the China Inland Mission been depending on its donors rather than on the living God the outcome might have been very far from what it was. But "God is equal to all emergencies," as Mr. Taylor loved to remind himself and others, and His dealings with the C. I. M. in the financial crisis of 1927 constitute one of the most marvelous answers to prayer that the Mission has ever known.

The following are the facts. The income of the Mission fell off in that one year not by thousands but by tens of thousands of dollars. With largely increased demands upon its resources, and with strict adherence to its principles of making no appeal for financial help and of never going into debt, how was the situation to be met—with an income diminished by no less than $114,000?

Yes, "God is equal to all emergencies"; and that year He was pleased to work in an unexpected way. Money transmitted to China from the home countries has to be changed into silver currency at a rate which is always fluctuating. But that year the fluctuation, strange to say, seemed steadily in favor of the Mission funds. More and more silver was purchasable with the money remitted from home, and by the close of the year it was found that while $114,000 *less* had been sent to China than in the previous year, the Mission had profited on exchange as much as $115,000! Thus all needs were met, and that year of special trial became one of overflowing praise.

And as to the matter of the closed door, Dr. Glover continues:

It was indeed a sad hour . . . and the outlook from the human point of view was dark enough. Would the door of missionary opportunity ever reopen? The question was variously answered . . . [by the skeptical, the worldly-wise, and the discouraged]. But there were missionaries—and those of the C. I. M. happily among the number—whose anointed eye saw the situation in a very different light.

That the blow came directly from Satan, and with intent to ruin the work of missions, they doubted not. But did the Word anywhere teach that God's servants were ever to accept defeat at the hands of Satan? Assuredly not. Had Satan at any time succeeded through persecution in destroying the cause of Christ? Far from it. . . . Paul, the great missionary, testified that the persecutions which befell him had *"fallen out rather unto the progress of the gospel,"* and he followed on to exhort his fellow-workers to be *"in nothing terrified by your adversaries."* Nothing in the New Testament missionary record is more impressive than the way opposition and persecution from the enemy were repeatedly made by God the very means of advancing the missionary enterprise. Every such assault of the adversary today, therefore, should become the occasion of a forward movement issuing in fresh expansion and enlarged results.

Now that is just the way the China Inland Mission was led to regard the adverse situation with which it was confronted. . . . Was missionary work in China at an end? How could it possibly be, with Christ's Great Commission unrevoked, and the task of giving the Gospel to China's millions still so very far from completed? At whatever cost, the work must go on. And so the Mission went upon its face before God in fervent prayer for the reopening of the door and for clear guidance as to its future plans.

Those were days of deep heart-searching, Dr. Glover goes on to testify, as well as of earnest prayer. And it was then, right in the midst of the trial, that God gave vision and conviction for a great advance. For it was then that, on the basis of a comprehensive

survey of the whole C. I. M. field, the leaders of the
Mission felt clearly led to appeal to God and His
people for, not one hundred, but *two hundred additional workers* for a forward movement of a
strongly evangelistic character.

Hardly could the constituency of the Mission at
home have been more rejoiced and impressed than
when this appeal was received. It was recognized
to be of God, the outcome of much prayer, and at
once new life began to be felt in all parts of the
work. The two years in which the new missionaries
were expected, not only asked for, passed quickly
(1929-31), and though faith was tried in various
ways, not least by strong counter attacks of the adversary in China, the story has been one of profound
encouragement and blessing.

Not only did 1931 witness the outgoing of the
last parties of the Two Hundred—ninety-one of
whom were from North America—but the provision
made for their reception in China was no less remarkable. The headquarters of the Mission in
Shanghai, which had long been inadequate for the
needs of the work, were replaced during that year
by the much larger, more suitable premises God has
provided without the cost of a single cent to the
Mission. An opportunity came, in answer to much
prayer, to sell the old premises for *sixty-five times
their original cost.* They had been the gift of a
member of the Mission now with the Lord, who
after more than forty years was thus enabled to

provide the new headquarters for the growing work just when they were so urgently needed.[2] And the new buildings were ready in time to receive the splendid parties of last fall, when over a hundred new workers arrived in China for the China Inland Mission in the brief period of one month.

Much more was included in that wonderful provision than the wisest leaders in the Mission could foresee. For when, early in the present year, the wholly unexpected attack was made upon Shanghai by Japanese forces, much of the fighting centered in and around the very district (Hongkew) in which the former headquarters of the China Inland Mission had been located. Just in time had the guiding hand of God led to the change which moved the Mission premises three miles farther back into the International Settlement, to a position of greater safety. Who but He could have foreseen and provided in this wonderful way to meet a situation so unexpected and acutely distressing?

Yes, He is caring still for the needs of His own work. Little wonder that the China Inland Mission stands foursquare on the old truths upon which it was founded; little wonder that it commemorates with thankfulness the centenary this year, 1932, of the birth of its father in God, the leader whose faith and obedience brought it into being. Thank God, there is not one of its twelve hundred and eighty-

[2]An additional gift from a retired American member of the Mission supplied admirable premises, also greatly needed, for Chinese workers and guests.

five missionaries who cannot and does not joyfully reiterate, today, the conviction of its founder:

The living God still lives, and the living Word *is* a living Word, and we may depend upon it. We may hang upon any word God ever spoke or caused by His Holy Spirit to be written.

> Oh, make but trial of His love;
>   Experience will decide
> How blest are they, and they alone,
>   Who in His truth confide.
>
> Fear Him, ye saints, and you will then
>   Have nothing else to fear;
> Make but His service your delight,
>   Your wants shall be His care.

EPILOGUE

NINETEEN EIGHTY-TWO will mark fifty years since the first edition of *Hudson Taylor's Spiritual Secret*. In their concluding chapter and Appendix the authors described how the human leadership of the China Inland Mission was passed on and how the principles laid down from the Mission's inception continued to be followed during the first twenty-five years after Hudson Taylor's death.

Fifty more years have now passed since this remarkable testimony to the faithfulness of God was first published. Through revolution, world war, and times as turbulent as any faced in the previous century, the Mission has again and again experienced God's power, provision, and protection. He has not changed.

China's spiritual need and claims have continued to challenge deeply dedicated young people from the West. Borden of Yale responded to the call of Muslim work in Northwest China. He died in Egypt on the way. At about the same time, J. O. Frazer, musician and engineer, was prayerfully laying the foundation for phenomenal church growth among the Lisu tribesmen in the southwestern borders of China. As a grim prelude to the testing by fire that the church in China would itself experience in the fifties and sixties, John and Betty Stam, from Albion, Michigan, fell as martyrs at the start of Mao's Long March.

The Japanese invasion of China and World War II forced many to leave their stations, and the CIM headquarters was temporarily moved from Shanghai to Chungking. The entire Chefoo school for missionaries' children was marched off to concentration camp. I shall never forget that march. Our teachers led us as we sang:

> God is our refuge and strength,
>   A very present help in trouble.
> Therefore will not we fear. . . .
>   The LORD of hosts is with us,
>   The God of Jacob is our refuge.*

Separated from parents for more than five years, many learned that God can be trusted.

But the greatest testing was yet to come. In the late forties the communist armies swept triumphantly southward. As Phyllis Thompson has so poignantly described in her book *China: The Reluctant Exodus,* following the communist victory the entire membership of the Mission was forced to leave China between 1949 and 1952. Cast upon God for guidance as Hudson Taylor had been on Brighton Beach eighty-six years earlier, leaders of the China Inland Mission met in Bournemouth, England. Once again in obedience and faith a momentous decision was made. All available personnel would be redeployed as the Mission launched forth in East Asia. With headquarters in Singapore, the new focus would be on Japan, Taiwan, Hong Kong, the Philippines, Thailand, Malaysia, Singapore, and Indonesia. Later Vietnam, Laos, Cambodia, and Korea would also be entered. For some countries the time was short, the harvest urgent. With the door to China firmly closed and grave suspicion of anything labeled "China" in many countries of Southeast Asia, the name China Inland Mission (CIM) gave place, albeit reluctantly, to Overseas Missionary Fellowship (OMF).

The new vision was "a church in every community and thereby the gospel to every creature." The approach was two-pronged. It recognized the strategic importance of Asia's burgeoning urban centers with their concentration of civil ser-

*Psalm 46:1, 7.

vants, students, and factory workers. At the same time neglected areas and hidden tribal groups, the "inlands" of East
Asia, were sought out. Church planting teams were sent in,
languages were reduced to writing, and the Bible translated. In
each field, theological education and literature ministries were
given high priority. In rural Thailand the Fellowship made its
major medical thrust with three hospitals and a leprosy control
program. Here, too, OMF later became deeply involved in
refugee ministries.

In 1965, CIM-OMF celebrated its centennial and prepared
for a new century. The Fellowship recognized with thanksgiving that a mature church was emerging in many countries of
East Asia. It longed to become a new instrument in partnership
with the churches in obedience to Christ's commission. The
result was the emergence of Home Councils in several Asian
countries where the vision of cross-cultural missions was
bright and growing. Now those Home Councils number seven.
Today the Overseas Missionary Fellowship increasingly serves
as a Fellowship where keen Christians from East and West
serve together as colleagues in response to God's sovereign
call. This new biblical partnership is only just beginning, but
the possibilities under God are almost limitless.

Finally, OMF is still deeply committed to the Chinese
people and can never forget that it came into existence as the
China Inland Mission. For thirty years the Fellowship has ac-
tively sought to call the church to prayer for our brothers and
sisters in China and to continue to proclaim the gospel through
radio broadcasts. Clearly God is at work in China today. The
Fellowship does not aspire to reimpose its former structures,
but it does long to learn from our brothers and sisters in China
and to respond to their initiatives in new dimensions of partnership in Christ's matchless service.

SINGAPORE, January 1981   JAMES HUDSON TAYLOR III

Every Christian reader is invited to join in the following prayer, which was written by a member of the China Inland Mission:

Send Thou, O Lord, to every place
   Swift messengers before Thy face,
The heralds of Thy wondrous grace,
   Where Thou, Thyself, wilt come.

Send men whose eyes have seen the King,
   Men in whose ears His sweet words ring,
Send such Thy lost ones home to bring:
   Send them where Thou wilt come —

To bring good news to souls in sin,
   The bruised and broken hearts to win,
In every place to bring them in,
   Where Thou, Thyself, wilt come.

Gird each one with the Spirit's sword,
   The sword of Thine own deathless Word,
And make them conquerors, conquering Lord,
   Where Thou, Thyself, wilt come.

Raise up, O Lord the Holy Ghost,
   From this broad land a mighty host,
Their war cry — We will seek the lost,
   Where Thou, O Christ, wilt come!

The past has not exhausted the possibilities nor the demands for doing great things for God. The church that is dependent on its past history for its miracles of power and grace is a fallen church. . . .

The greatest benefactor this age could have is the man who will bring the teachers and the church back to prayer.

E. M. Bounds, in *Power Through Prayer*

CHRONOLOGICAL OUTLINE

1832, May 21.	James Hudson Taylor born in Barnsley, Yorkshire, England.
1849, June.	Conversion, followed by call to life service.
1850, May.	Beginning medical studies in Hull as assistant to Dr. Robert Hardey.
1853, September 19.	Sailed for China, as an agent of the Chinese Evangelization Society.
1850-1864.	The Taiping Rebellion.
1854, March 1.	Hudson Taylor landed in Shanghai.
1854-1855.	Ten evangelistic journeys.
1855, Oct.-Nov.	First home "inland": six weeks on the island of Tsungming.
1855-1856.	Seven months with the Rev. William C. Burns.
1856, October.	Settlement at Ningpo.
1857, June.	Resignation from the Chinese Evangelization Society
1858, January 20.	Marriage to Miss Maria J. Dyer.

1859, September.	Undertook charge of Dr. Parker's hospital, Ningpo.
1860, Summer.	Return to England on first furlough.
1860-1865.	Hidden years.
1865, June 25.	Surrender at Brighton, and prayer for twenty-four fellow-workers for inland China.
1866, May 26.	Sailed with the first party of the China Inland Mission, on the "Lammermuir"—a four months' journey.
1866, December.	Settlement of the Lammermuir Party in Hangchow.
1867, August 23.	Death of little Gracie.
1868, August 22.	The Yangchow Riot.
1869, September 4.	Entered into The Exchanged Life:—"God has made me a new man!"
1870, June 21.	The Tientsin Massacre.
1870, July 23.	Death of Mrs. Hudson Taylor (*nee* Dyer).
1872, March.	Retirement of Mr. W. Berger.
1872, August 6.	Formation of the London Council of the China Inland Mission.
1872, October 9.	Return to China with Mrs. Taylor (*nee* Faulding).
1874, January 27.	Recorded prayer for pioneer missionaries for the nine unevangelized provinces.

1874, June.	Opening, with Mr. Judd, the western branch of the Mission in Wuchang.
1874, July 26.	Death of Miss Emily Blatchley.
1874-1875, Winter.	The Lowest Ebb: Mr. Taylor laid aside in England, paralyzed.
1875, January.	Appeal for prayer for eighteen pioneers for the nine unevangelized provinces.
1876, September 13.	Signing of the Chefoo Convention.
1876-1878.	Widespread evangelistic journeys throughout inland China.
1878, Autumn.	Mrs. Hudson Taylor leads the advance of women missionaries to the far interior.
1879, Autumn.	Mrs. George Nicoll and Mrs. G. W. Clarke pioneer the way for women's work in western China.
1881, May.	Death of Mrs. George King, at Hanchung.
1881, November.	The appeal for The Seventy (Wuchang).
1885, February 5.	Going out of The Cambridge Party.
1886, November 13-26.	First meeting of the China Council, and appeal for The Hundred (Anking).
1887, December.	Visit to England of Mr. Henry W. Frost, inviting Mr. Taylor to the United States.

1888, Summer.	Mr. Taylor's first visit to North America.
1889, October.	The widest outlook of his life: *To Every Creature*.
1889, November.	First visits to Sweden, Norway, and Denmark.
1890, August.	First visit to Australia.
1900, May.	Beginning of the "Boxer" outbreak.
1900, August.	Mr. D. E. Hoste appointed as Acting General Director.
1902, November.	Mr. Taylor resigned Directorate to Mr. D. E. Hoste.
1904, July 30.	Mrs. Hudson Taylor's death in Switzerland.
1905, February.	Mr. Taylor's return to China on last visit.
1905, June 3.	Home-call, from Hunan.

Moody Press, a ministry of the Moody Bible Institute, is designed for education, evangelization and edification. If we may assist you in knowing more about Christ and the Christian life, please write us without obligation to: Moody·Press, c/o MLM, Chicago, Illinois 60610.